SNOWSHOE ROUTES

Adirondacks
& Catskills

SNOWSHOE ROUTES

Adirondacks & Catskills

BILL INGERSOLL

THE MOUNTAINEERS BOOKS

THE MOUNTAINEERS BOOKS
*is the nonprofit publishing arm of The Mountaineers Club, an organization
founded in 1906 and dedicated to the exploration, preservation, and
enjoyment of outdoor and wilderness areas.*

1001 SW Klickitat Way, Suite 201, Seattle, WA 98134

Manufactured in the United States of America

Acquiring Editor: Christine Hosler
Project Editors: Laura Drury and Margaret Sullivan
Copy Editor: Colin Chisholm
Cover and Book Design: The Mountaineers Books
Layout: Mayumi Thompson
Cartographer: Moore Creative Design
Photographer: All photos by the author unless otherwise noted

Cover photograph: *Woman and dog running in snow* © Corbis
Frontispiece: *Climbing towards the treeline on Mount Marcy*

Contents

The Northern Catskills

The Burroughs Range

Western Catskill Mountains, Valleys, and Lakes

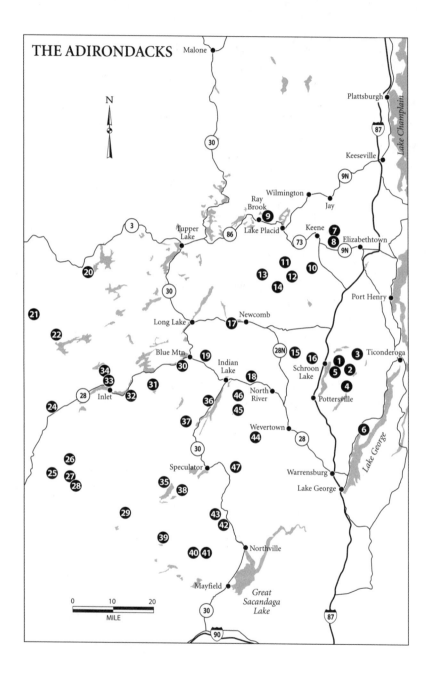

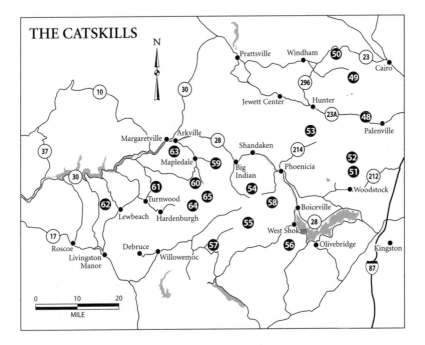

Quick Reference to the Trails

Trail number and name	Distance (miles)	Hiking time (hours)	Family friendly	Panoramic views	Camping possibilities	Difficulty rating	Comments
1 Goose Pond	3	1–2	X			Easy	Scenic pond with mountain views
2 Pharaoh Mountain	9.4	6		X	X	Difficult	Trail to mountain passes several lakes
3 Short Swing Trail	11.2	48	X		X	Moderate	Ponds, lean-tos, and views of rugged mountains
4 Pharaoh Lake from the South	7.2	3–4	X	X	X	Moderate	Popular trek to large wilderness lake
5 Spectacle Pond	3.4	1–2	X	X	X	Easy	Outstanding views
6 Fifth Peak	5.4	3	X	X	X	Moderate	Views of Lake George
7 Lost Pond and Weston Mountain	4.8	4		X	X	Moderate/Difficult	High-elevation mountain plateau
8 Hurricane Mountain	5.6	3	X	X	X	Moderate	Open summit with 360-degree view
9 Haystack Mounain	6.6	4–5		X		Difficult	Easily accessible from Lake Placid and Saranac Lake
10 Lower Wolf Jaw	10.4	8		X		Most Difficult	Deceptively difficult climb!
11 Avalanche Pass	9.2	5	X	X	X	Moderate	Extremely popular hike with outstanding mountain views
12 Mount Marcy from Upper Works	20.6	48		X	X	Most Difficult	Multiday expedition to New York's highest peak
13 Duck Hole via the Preston Ponds	11	6–8		X		Difficult	Trek across a series of frozen lakes
14 Mount Adams	4.6	3–4		X	X	Difficult	Fire tower with view of Mount Marcy and the High Peaks
15 Bailey Pond	2.4	1–2	X		X	Easy	Short hike to scenic pond
16 Big Pond	3.2	2	X		X	Easy	Chance for easy side trip to heron rookery site
17 Goodnow Mountain	3.4	2–3	X	X		Moderate	Restored fire tower
18 Ross, Whortleberry, and Big Bad Luck Ponds	8.1	4–6	X		X	Moderate	Collection of interesting lakes
19 Tirrell Pond	9.2	5–6	X	X	X	Moderate	Lake with two lean-tos
20 Cat Mountain Pond	11.2	6		X	X	Moderate	Pond at the foot of rugged cliffs
21 West Branch Oswegatchie Headwaters	11	8			X	Most Difficult	Trek through remote wilderness

Trail number and name	Distance (miles)	Hiking time (hours)	Family friendly	Panoramic views	Camping possibilities	Difficulty rating	Comments
22 Wilderness Lakes Tract	10	5–7			X	Difficult	Trek across a series of lakes
23 Whetstone Gulf	5	3	X	X		Easy/Moderate	Interesting canyon in the Tug Hill region
24 Middle Settlement Lake	6.4	3–4	X		X	Moderate	Popular year-round hike
25 Stone Dam Lake	7	3–4	X		X	Moderate	Secluded pond on the edge of the Adirondack Park
26 Little Woodhull Lake	6.6	3–4	X			Moderate	One of the author's favorites
27 Twin Lakes	6.4	3	X		X	Moderate	Site of historic dam
28 Cotton Lake	7	4			X	Difficult	Exploration of old roads
29 DeBraine and Trout Lakes	5.2	3			X	Difficult	Old growth forest between lakes
30 Wilson Pond	5.8	3	X		X	Moderate	Great lean-to for winter camping
31 Sagamore Lake Loop	3.9	2	X			Easy	Loop around historic Great Camp
32 Mohegan Lake	10.4	5–6			X	Moderate	Hike to secluded Great Camp
33 Cascade Lake	2.6	2	X		X	Easy	Hike along wide old road to scenic lake
34 Queer Lake Loop	9.7	6	X		X	Moderate	Old growth forest
35 T Lake	7.2	4	X		X	Moderate	Great backcountry hike
36 Snowy Mountain	7.4	6		X		Difficult	Highest mountain in the southern Adirondacks
37 Sucker Brook–Colvin Brook Trail	16	48		X	X	Most Difficult	Expedition into remote wilderness
38 Buckhorn Lake	3	1–2	X		X	Easy	Wilderness setting within easy reach
39 Good Luck Mountain	4.4	3	X	X		Difficult	Views from interesting cliffs
40 The County Line Lakes	7+	6+			X	Most Difficult	Expedition into remote wilderness
41 Chase Lake	5.2	2–3	X		X	Moderate	Scenic but seldom-visited lake
42 Groff Creek	4.4	2–3	X		X	Moderate	Beautiful hemlock forest
43 Vly Creek and Southerland Mountain	6	6		X	X	Most Difficult	Off-trail journey to scenic mountain
44 Siamese Ponds from Eleventh Mountain	13.2	7	X		X	Moderate	Over a mountain and along a river to remote ponds
45 Puffer Pond and Twin Ponds	6.5	6			X	Difficult	Potential multiday trek into remote wilderness
46 Clear Pond	2.6	1–2	X		X	Easy	Scenic pond near Indian Lake village
47 Extract Brook	4.6	3			X	Difficult	Year-round access across East Branch Sacandaga River

Trail number and name	Distance (miles)	Hiking time (hours)	Family friendly	Panoramic views	Camping possibilities	Difficulty rating	Comments
48 Sunset Rock and Inspiration Point	3	1–2	X	X		Easy	Mountain views with little climbing involved
49 Blackhead Mountain Loop	5.2	4		X	X	Most Difficult	Loop hike over rugged mountain
50 Windham High Peak	6.6	3–4	X	X	X	Moderate	Easiest of the High Peaks
51 Overlook Mountain	5	2	X	X		Moderate	Fire tower and historic ruins
52 Echo Lake via Overlook Mountain	9	4	X	X	X	Moderate	Secluded pond with lean-to
53 Hunter Mountain via Notch Lake	7.6	5		X	X	Difficult	Rugged climb to 4000-foot summit
54 Giant Ledge and Panther Mountain	6.6	4–5	X	X		Moderate	Scenic cliff tops
55 East Branch Neversink River	2.8+	1–2+			X	Difficult	Access to remote wilderness valley
56 Ashokan High Point	9	4–5	X	X		Moderate	Loop trail with moderate grades
57 Red Hill Fire Tower	3.8	2	X	X		Easy	Fire tower summit
58 Wittenberg	7.8	5		X		Difficult	Most scenic of the High Peaks
59 Balsam Mountain Loop	5.2	3–4	X	X	X	Moderate	Loop hike with moderate grades
60 Balsam Lake Mountain Fire Tower	6	3	X	X		Moderate	Fire tower summit
61 Alder Lake Loop	2	1–2	X	X		Easy	Site of historic lodge
62 Huggins Lake	3.8	1–2	X			Easy	Secluded pond
63 Dry Brook Ridge	8.2	4–5		X		Moderate	Lightly used trail to great views
64 Headwaters of the Beaver Kill	6.5+	3–4 minimum			X	Difficult	Trek into remote wilderness
65 Doubletop from the Beaver Kill	11+	8			X	Most Difficult	Trailless High Peak

Acknowledgments

I began hiking and snowshoeing as a solitary pursuit, but over the years I have developed a network of knowledgeable and enthusiastic companions whose love for the Adirondacks and Catskills is no less fervent than my own. I availed myself of their company whenever the opportunity presented itself. In particular, I would like to thank Paul and Liz Kalac, Paul Repak, Paul Sirtoli, Jennifer Sweeney, and Doug Tinkler, all of whom accompanied me at one time or another during the winter when I performed the principal "research" for this book. These companions not only enlivened the walks, but their observations and insights augmented my own.

The Kalacs deserve further credit, for it was they who hiked Snowy Mountain at a time when it looked as though my own ambitious hiking schedule would not allow me to get there before winter's end. As Paul and I reasoned, what good is an Adirondack snowshoeing guidebook that doesn't include a mountain named Snowy? They climbed the mountain on Liz's birthday, and it was Paul's notes of that trip that formed the basis for the trail description in this guide.

I also owe thanks to the editors and staff at The Mountaineers Books for making this project happen. I hope that this has been a pleasant experience for all involved.

Above all, however, I would be remiss if I did not mention Barbara McMartin's indirect contributions to this book. It was her trail descriptions that originally introduced and enticed me to many portions of the Adirondacks, and it was the historical research she provided in her guidebooks that formed the basis of my own understanding of why the region is the way it is today. And, of course, it was Barbara who got me into the guidebook business in the first place. Writing *Snowshoe Routes* has given me the chance to structure my first "solo" book from the ground up—using my own voice and my own observations from my many trips over the years—although I found it impossible to distance myself very far from Barbara's influence. The reader will find that influence everywhere in this guide. She passed away in 2005, before I had finished drafting the manuscript.

To everyone who contributed, thank you.

Introduction

Snowshoeing has been an integral part of New York's mountain landscapes as long as people have been traversing these wild spaces in winter. The name of Raquette Lake is said to be derived from the pile of discarded snowshoes left on its shores by Loyalist officers fleeing to Canada during the Revolutionary War, and for many decades later woods-wise trappers used snowshoes while manning their long, solitary trap lines.

However, snowshoeing as an act enjoyable for its own sake never caught on the way Nordic skiing did. The author T. Morris Longstreth, while praising the ability of snowshoes to help their wearers ascend rugged mountains in the deepest snows, wrote: "Snow-shoes may not be an invention of the devil, but certainly of an irreverent god. The sight of our divine form a-waddle is a spectacle for mirth." Skiing, with its swift and graceful glides, was and always has been perceived as an art; snowshoeing, on the other hand, was utilitarian.

Nevertheless, a recent trend has seen a number of frustrated winter travelers put away their skis in favor of the freedom that snowshoeing offers. While cross-country skis have their advantages, they also have distinct limitations. One is the level of maintenance that some skis require, but I think that the most critical limitation is that of terrain.

Cross-country skiing works best on well-maintained trails with wide treads and long sightlines, but the benefits begin to fall off sharply when one actually tries to take them cross country. This is not an issue for people who are attracted to the sheer exhilaration of gliding along a woodland trail or across a frozen lake, but it is a serious setback for the winter explorer whose primary pleasure is in reaching secluded and unique places—people who want to get off the well-groomed trails and really see the backcountry.

This migration from skiing to snowshoeing has been facilitated by the complete modernization of snowshoe design in recent decades. Rather than the cumbersome wood-frame "rackets" that the old fur-trappers wore—the design responsible for the waddling gait that Longstreth criticized—most of today's snowshoers use the aluminum-frame design that have transformed snowshoes into narrow, lightweight tools that are perfectly effective in crossing the most rugged terrain the North Woods have to offer.

The design has been so simplified, in fact, that there is no technique for the novice to learn, no special stride to master. Waddling is a thing of the past. People who enjoy hiking in the summer—and who are loathe to give up their explorations in the winter just because of a little snow—have found snowshoes to be the best way to get around in the woods from December to March, when snow covers the trails. There are no limitations in terrain, and if anything snowshoeing offers more freedom than summer hiking—freedom from black flies and crowds, and the freedom to cross frozen ponds and wetlands. There are few places you can *not* get to on snowshoes.

THE ADIRONDACK AND CATSKILL MOUNTAINS

While you can snowshoe anywhere in New York's snow belt, few people need directions to their local parks. I have therefore written this guidebook for the people who really want to get out and enjoy the unique, wide-open spaces of the Adirondack and Catskill parks in winter—places where snowshoes are not just a toy to play with, but a necessity for getting around.

The summit of Hurricane Mountain

The dimensions of the Adirondack Park are breathtaking to consider: at 6 million acres, you would have to go to Alaska to find a larger park in the United States. Of that total, 2.3 million acres are state-owned Forest Preserve lands, protected from lumbering and development by Article XIV of the state constitution. Just over a million acres of the Forest Preserve are designated as wilderness areas—places where all motorized forms of access, including snowmobiles, are legally banned. The Adirondacks represent the largest collection of public lands in the crowded Northeast.

The term "Adirondack Mountains" is often used to describe this region, but to characterize the entire park simply as one large mountain range is misleading. The long western fringe, for instance, has no mountains per se at all. Where the topography *is* distinctly mountainous, the mountains do not easily arrange themselves into "ranges" as do other mountain groups, like the Rockies, the Sierra, the Cascades, or the Appalachians. A few mountains are aligned into long chains, but most are thrown willy-nilly across the map wherever chance happened to place them.

This has to do with the origin of the mountains, which, unlike the neighboring Appalachians, are still rising. The rocks that compose the Adirondacks may be among the oldest on the North American continent, but the mountains as we see them today are growing as fast as 1 millimeter a year. This is because of an unknown geological force deep within the earth that is placing pressure on the planet's crust and forcing it upward, creating a round, dome-like plateau that radiates rivers in all directions of the compass.

Even more impressive than the region's topography is its hydrology: 5 principle watersheds, 3000 lakes and ponds, and 30,000 miles of streams and rivers, for anyone keeping count. For the most part, it was the last ice age that contributed this gift of water to the landscape. With the ancient bedrock so close to the surface, water cannot simply soak into the ground out of sight. It forms pools in the hollows of the rock, and streams and cascades along the fault lines. These waterways are just as "Adirondack" as the mountains.

There is also the natural community to consider. The defining element is the forest cover—densely wooded, where the boreal zones of Canada mix and harmonize with the more "southern" sugar maple, hemlock, and white pine. All animal species in the Adirondacks are by necessity forest dwellers: moose, white-tailed deer, coyotes, hares, martens, and bobcats, to name a few. Moose were completely exterminated from the Adirondacks in the nineteenth century, but in one of the region's most triumphant success stories, these emblems of the North Woods have been wandering back on their own since the 1980s, probably coming in from Vermont across a frozen Lake Champlain.

There is a fourth factor to consider when trying to describe what the

Adirondacks "are." Make no mistake, Adirondack Park is a place of cultural significance as well as wild beauty. Unlike national parks, more than half of the Adirondacks are privately owned, with about 150,000 year-round residents and perhaps just as many summer residents. This is a place where people live and work, with an economy based as much on logging as tourism. Adirondackers have created distinct art forms and architectural styles, and the lore that they have passed down over the decades has filled dozens of books. This, too, is what we refer to when we say "Adirondack."

The Catskill Park shares many of the political peculiarities of its neighbor to the north: its publicly-owned portion is also part of the Forest Preserve, and the remainder is privately owned. Like the Adirondacks, there is some behind-the-scenes tension between those who are making their living in the mountains year-round and those who are coming just for the scenery.

But there the similarities end, for the Catskill landscape is worlds apart from the Adirondacks. The rocks are sedimentary in origin, layered atop one another in bands that sometimes make the mountainsides look like stepped pyramids. These mountains do form distinct ranges, and in fact there are few stand-alone peaks. While there are many streams and several reservoirs, there are very few natural ponds. The forests are decidedly "southern" in nature, with a preponderance of hardwoods and with boreal stands of balsam fir capping only the highest peaks.

The Catskill region lacks the grand scale of the Adirondacks, and its wild spaces are notably smaller. However, at one point the mountains had been so deforested for farming and harvesting tanbark that very little of the wild survived. Proximity to the Hudson River and large metropolitan areas made the area vulnerable to cultivation and exploitation at a much earlier date. Stone fences from the old settlements can still be traced high up the mountainsides, although the fields and pastures have long since returned to forest. It is amusing to consider—as you snowshoe up some of the mountain trails—that these routes were originally created for farmers leading their cattle to market.

The legacy of this era is a relatively high density of roads and a fragmentation of the forest. An Adirondacker sojourning in the Catskills misses the sheer open space preserved simply by virtue of its excessiveness. In the Catskills, the forestland that found its way into state ownership was primarily the rugged mountain terrain that had little commercial or residential value. Human works are so entrenched within the broad, fertile valleys between the mountains that there are few wild spaces there.

What you will find in the Catskills is a very attractive and well laid out trail system. Hiking trails interconnect with such variety that it is easy to plan loop trips and through trips up and over the mountains. The trails lead to small ledges with tremendous views, to the sites of the luxurious nineteenth-century mountain houses, and into a handful of secluded valleys.

THE ADIRONDACKS AND CATSKILLS IN WINTER

These two mountain regions are among the snowiest regions in the state. They are subject to storms from both Lake Ontario to the west and the Atlantic Ocean to the southeast. Since they are thrust well above the outlying valleys, there are few storm systems that manage to pass by without unloading some amount of snow. Often the Hudson and Mohawk valleys may see only meager amounts of snowfall while the upland areas can be buried under several feet.

Typically, the snowshoeing season begins around Christmas and New Year's, and it extends through the end of March. Winter is a notoriously unpredictable season, though, and so the snow cannot be expected to come and go at any set dates. Snowshoeing may begin in early December and last into April, especially in the more northerly Adirondacks, but there have been several recent winters that have seen meager snowfalls and early springs.

I picked the sixty-five routes for this guide based on their accessibility in winter. All of them start from plowed roadways, although not all of them have plowed trailheads. In fair weather, any car can drive to any of these snowshoe routes. However, any lake-effect shower or nor'easter can easily render the many

Beech saplings on Balsam Mountain

town roads in both regions temporarily impassable to two-wheel-drive vehicles. Plow crews are pretty vigilant about keeping their roads clear, but trailheads are a secondary priority. If it snows on the weekend, these parking areas may not be cleared out until later in the week. Therefore, even where this guide mentions the presence of a plowed, maintained trailhead parking area, be prepared to have to shovel out a spot for your car if it has snowed recently. Never park in the path of the plows.

Snow conditions in the woods can vary greatly not only from week to week but also from day to day and even hour to hour, and the quality of the snow can have a direct impact on your snowshoeing experience. The best snow for walking involves a soft, fresh layer over a harder base. Too much fresh snow can bog you down, and too much hard snow can speed up the wear and tear on your snowshoes. A wet, heavy snow will develop on a mild day. There is really no way to predict the kind of snow you will find in the woods until you get there.

The hiking times given in this guidebook assume normal walking conditions, but the actual walking times may be considerably longer if the snow conditions are not favorable. Groups may fare better in that they can rotate who has to break trail. Some trails—particularly those in the High Peaks regions of both parks—are well used enough that they may already have a good base packed down by previous snowshoers. However, many other trails see only inconsistent use and will likely have no such base.

ENJOYING THE FOREST PRESERVE: RESPONSIBLE USE

Nearly all of the snowshoe routes listed in this book are located in the Forest Preserves of the Adirondack and Catskill parks. The New York State Department of Environmental Conservation (NYS DEC or simply DEC) is responsible for the management of these constitutionally protected lands.

Use of the Forest Preserve is governed by the two principal land classifications, wild forest and wilderness. In wild forest areas, snowshoers may encounter a wider variety of trail use and design, including snowmobile trails. Wilderness areas are managed to provide chances for solitude and to preserve natural communities. This guide makes use of both types of management areas, for besides the snowmobiles there is little difference between the two in winter. With very few exceptions, the routes in this book avoid the snowmobile trails in favor of the quieter recesses of the forest.

Official DEC-maintained trails are marked with colored plastic disks, which will be either red, yellow, or blue. These markers can sometimes be covered in snow, but for the most part they are easy to spot.

This guide also makes use of unofficial trails or paths, which may not be marked at all. Such routes are simply a matter of tradition—they may not appear on any maps and they are not maintained by DEC. There is also an abundance of long-abandoned woods roads in these mountains, and they often make exceptional snowshoe routes. Using any of these unofficial trails requires basic navigation skills on the part of the snowshoer.

A few routes described in this book make no use of trails of any kind. These off-trail scrambles are called "bushwhacks," and these should be reserved for the experts only. Bushwhacking is generally regarded as being much easier in winter than summer, when snow covers the underbrush and preserves your tracks all the way back to your car, so that on the return you have a custom-made path to follow. Attempting one of these trips requires strong navigational skills as well as a sense of adventure. Always let someone at home know your intended route before striking off for the woods.

While individual places within the Forest Preserve may have specific regulations for public use, the following guidelines apply to most regions:
- Use only dead and down wood for fires. It is illegal (and in poor taste) to cut any standing timber, even if it is no longer living.
- Carry out what you carry in.
- Camp at least 150 feet from the nearest trail, road, or source of water, unless the site is designated by a yellow "camp here" disk.
- Permits are required for stays of three or more nights in a single location, or for groups of more than eight people. They are available from the nearest forest ranger. Contact the appropriate DEC office for more information.

In addition to the above, the following regulations apply to the High Peaks Wilderness in the Adirondacks:
- Camping is permitted only at designated sites and lean-tos in the area surrounding Flowed Lands, Lake Colden, and Marcy Dam, and at all places above 3500 feet in elevation.
- Camping is prohibited above 4000 feet at any time of the year, to protect the fragile alpine environments.
- Campfires are banned at all locations east of Indian Pass.
- Use of skis or snowshoes is mandatory when snow covers the trail, even on well-packed trails. Avoid leaving "post holes" in the trail that will ruin the packed surface.
- Dogs must be leashed while on trails, at campsites, on mountain summits, and wherever people have gathered.
- All glass containers are prohibited.
- Bear-resistant canisters are required for the storage of all food, food containers, garbage, and toiletries for overnight camping from April 1 to

November 30. While bears are not active during the winter, other animals such as pine martens, fishers, squirrels, and chipmunks may all be happy to relieve you of some of your supplies while natural food sources are lean. Therefore, these canisters are recommended throughout the year.

The following applies only to the Catskill Forest Preserve:
- Camping is permitted above 3500 feet only during the winter months.

ICE CROSSINGS

One of the advantages to winter traveling is the ability to travel freely across frozen ponds and wetlands, thereby allowing the snowshoer to appreciate the wilderness landscape in a way impossible in summer. Different people have different attitudes about this, however, and some are reluctant to consider ice crossings at all.

Generally speaking, ponds will be safely frozen by mid-January or earlier, and they begin to thaw by late March. Good ice will appear white or light gray, and weak ice will be bluish or dark gray. Areas around inlets and outlets often do not freeze at all and should always be avoided.

Trekking across Sunshine Pond

Streams freeze inconsistently. Those at the highest elevations usually do ice up on an annual basis, as do certain other streams throughout the region. Most freeze enough to form ice bridges that are very capable of supporting snowshoers. Others defy the odds and never freeze. Large rivers will only freeze during the coldest winters and rarely before mid-February. In the more southerly Catskills, streams are much more reluctant to freeze, and many may remain running throughout the winter.

The simplest way to test ice is to tap it firmly with a ski pole or walking stick. Tapping solid ice will sound much like tapping a block of wood. While making the crossing, have the members of your group spread out so that the weight is distributed. When crossing a stream, cross one at a time.

These are just basic guidelines to consider. Indeed, if you do not feel comfortable crossing a sheet of ice, then do not feel compelled to do so. While getting wet feet may be merely an inconvenience in the summer, it has the potential to become a very serious health risk in the winter. Staying dry should be your primary concern. I have made an effort to point out in the text where certain stream crossings could be an issue; use your own discretion in deciding whether (or how) to cross them.

For ponds and lakes, I have included a few routes that deliberately cross the ice, where doing so enhances the experience or makes a significant shortcut. All of these by default have earned "difficult" trail ratings, highlighting the fact that such routes are not for novices. However, most of the routes described in this book do not have such requirements. They may take you to the edge of a secluded pond or around its shoreline, but the option to cross on the ice will be entirely up to you.

CHOOSING A SNOWSHOE

There are a number of basic snowshoe designs, but the one best suited to travel in the Adirondacks and Catskills is the simple "bear paw," with an oval frame and no tail. Most of the modern snowshoes are a modified version of the bear paw. However, within this basic design there are a variety of features that can affect the comfort, effectiveness, and longevity of your snowshoes.

The most important features to look for are crampons, or steel spikes, under the toe and heel plates. You will want your snowshoes to do more than just float on the snow—you will want them to grip the snow, especially on hills. Several entry-level snowshoes do not have crampons, and these are probably only suitable for city parks. For even the easiest hikes in this guide, you will need crampons built into your snowshoes.

Next, consider what size snowshoe you will need. The longer the snowshoe, the more weight it can carry and the better its buoyancy; but a snowshoe that

Snowshoer on Mount Adams

is too long for its wearer will be cumbersome. Consider what types of trips you expect to be using them for, too. If you only intend to take shorter hikes along well-traveled trails, then you may do fine with smaller snowshoes. However, if you plan to travel in more rugged country, you will need a longer pair. Manufacturers rate their snowshoes according to the wearer's body weight, and if you are a backpacker remember to factor in the weight of your pack.

A key consideration for many people is the binding system, or the set of straps that hold the snowshoes to your feet. There are a number of different mechanisms that manufacturers use, and all have their advantages and disadvantages. My experience has been that plastic ratcheting straps, while easier to lock and unlock, have a tendency to come undone by themselves, usually in the middle of the trail. Nylon straps are better at staying in place, but they can also get wet and freeze in position. Therefore, in my opinion, no binding system is perfect.

Durability is a major factor to consider for any snowshoe. Remember, these are things that you are going to be pounding into the snow with your full body weight step after step. Wear and tear is inevitable, and it will take the form of missing frame straps, popped rivets, and worn decking or webbing. Some manufacturers offer competitive warranties—it pays to shop around.

FOOTWEAR

Keeping your feet warm, dry, and comfortable is of paramount concern in winter. Therefore, it is important to choose wisely the type of boots you wear on your snowshoe treks.

Snowshoes can be strapped to just about any type of boot, including summer hiking boots and the bigger, bulkier pack boots. Do *not* use anything that is not watertight. If you use your summer hiking boots, you will also need gaiters and insulated socks. Is there room inside the boot for this extra bulk? If you have to cram your sock-covered feet inside, then they will sweat the entire time and potentially make things worse for yourself.

Boots that come midway up your shin are well adapted to deep snow. They offer good ankle support, and if tucked under your snow pants will prevent snow from getting in. Otherwise, gaiters may be required to keep the snow out of your boots.

WINTER CLOTHING

The key to dressing for a winter hike is to dress in *layers*. Keeping warm and comfortable in winter is a matter of managing your body's own ability to generate heat, and if you are wearing one big, bulky coat you will not be able to do this. You will be too warm with it on, and too cold with it off.

Depending on how warm or cold the air is, I can be wearing anywhere from two to five layers of clothing on my torso while snowshoeing. These layers begin with synthetic long underwear, which wick moisture away from my skin. Over this I wear a wool or fleece shirt, with breast pockets for my camera and headlamp. Next I wear a wool sweater, a thin wool jacket, and then a shell jacket to repel the elements. This is what I wear when the weather is rough and cold, but on milder days I can add and subtract these layers to adjust to almost any condition.

For my lower body, I typically wear three layers: synthetic long underwear, synthetic hiking pants, and wool snow pants.

This is what I have found works for me, but these are not the only types of clothing and material available. The key is to avoid wearing cotton clothing—if you have any, do yourself a favor and leave it in your closet. When cotton gets wet, it loses its insulating ability and dries slowly, making it useless as outdoor clothing. Wearing it greatly increases the risk for hypothermia in any season, and in winter it can be especially dangerous.

On the other hand, any of the synthetic materials, as well as wool and fleece, work well. Be wary of "waterproof" clothing—yes, it may keep airborne moisture out, but it also locks perspiration in. Look for clothing that is either breathable or that can be ventilated.

Scarves and facemasks are indispensable in bitterly cold weather, as are sunglasses on sunny days, when the reflected light from a frozen lake can be blinding. Gloves will give you greater dexterity, but mittens are better at keeping your fingers warm.

When snowshoeing, always be attuned to how your body feels—if you are sweating or feel too cool, stop and adjust your layers.

OTHER GEAR

Many snowshoers like to walk with ski poles for balance. They do have their usefulness, but they are not a necessity, as they are for cross-country skiing.

One peculiarity about winter hiking is that your drinking water tends to freeze while riding in your pack. The easiest way around this is to fill your water bottles with hot water before setting off. Storing your bottles in insulated pouches—or nestling them within your spare clothing—will help them further resist freezing.

Cold temperatures will suck the life out of batteries. This will impact a number of items that hikers routinely bring into the woods, including cameras, flashlights, and GPS units. Keep the batteries, if the not the device itself, close to your body if you want them to remain reliable throughout the day.

In addition to these suggestions, it is important to get acquainted with the following list of essential items to carry in your pack.

THE TEN ESSENTIALS

1. Navigation: Carry a map and compass for the area you plan to travel in, and know how to use them.
2. Sun protection: This is an especially important consideration when crossing a frozen lake or any expanse of open snow, where the reflected sunlight can be painful to unprotected eyes.
3. Insulation: Not only dress in layers but also bring extra clothing—particularly socks and gloves—in case what you are wearing becomes wet.
4. Illumination: Because winter days are so short, it is simply unwise to venture into the wilderness without a flashlight or headlamp. Remember, in late December darkness arrives by 5:00 PM, and so what we normally consider mid-afternoon is actually very late in the day for snowshoeing purposes. It is extremely easy for even experienced hikers to misjudge the time and come out of the woods later than expected. One of the benefits

of winter hiking is that you can follow your tracks back to the trailhead even after dark, but this advantage is null and void if you do not have a source of light!

5. First aid supplies: Packable kits are widely available, and they are indispensable. Take advantage of first-aid classes in your area to learn not only how to treat injuries but also how to recognize the symptoms of hypothermia and frostbite.

6. Fire: Always carry waterproof matches or matches in a waterproof container. If someone in your party is showing signs of hypothermia, keeping the person warm will be your topmost concern.

7. Repair kit and tools: What you don't have will likely be the one thing you need the most. A good knife is the most useful item you can have in your pack, as is a "multi-tool" with a pair of pliers. Parachute cord, duct tape, and even hand-held riveters are all things you might find useful while snowshoeing.

8. Nutrition: Bring not just a lunch for day trips but also snacks to keep you going. For overnights, pack at least one extra day's worth of food.

9. Hydration: For day trips, carry at least two quarts of drinking water. It is better to carry more than you think you will need. For camping trips, boiling water may be the only effective way to treat water for drinking—water filters freeze after the first use.

10. Emergency shelter: See the next section.

WINTER CAMPING

Winter camping, if done properly, can be a very comfortable and rewarding experience, but the margin of error is far less forgiving than summer camping. The intent of this book is to point out places where camping is appropriate and enjoyable to those with experience, but it is not intended to be a primer for those who have never camped in the winter before. If you are contemplating spending your first night in the woods, do not go alone. Join an outdoor recreation club, hire a guide, or seek the company of someone with practical experience. What follows are some general things to consider for a winter camping trip.

Having the right sleeping bag is essential, for it is this more than anything else that will retain your body heat for a sustained period. Manufacturers rate their sleeping bags by temperature ranges, and so what works in summer may be a failure in winter. When selecting a sleeping bag, pick one with a temperature rating well below the overnight temperatures you expect to be sleeping through. In other words, even if you do not intend to camp in weather colder than 0°F, pick one rated for -20°F anyway. You do not want to be pushing the limits of your bag when the temperature actually does reach 0°F.

Winter campsite at Cat Mountain Pond

There are a number of winter-specific tents to choose from, from so-called four-season tents to several more customized designs made for the avid winter campers. These are all valid choices. Four-season tents are essentially the same as the three-season tents you use in summer, except that they are modified to withstand a winter storm. They have additional poles for withstanding a burden of snow, and the fly wraps farther around the tent to keep out the wind. If you intend to weather a major snowstorm on your backpacking trip, bring a four-season tent.

Otherwise, a three-season tent in good repair will work fine in winter. The purpose of a tent is to provide shelter, not warmth. Remember to keep it well ventilated—do not zip up all the flaps! The amount of moisture that can accumulate inside a closed-up tent through perspiration is staggering, enough to dampen your gear considerably.

A tent can be easily set up on top of the snow. Begin by packing down a camping area with your snowshoes. Then spread out a tarp or watertight ground cloth, and set the tent up on top of that. Place another watertight sheet inside the tent. Remember, as you lay inside, your body heat will be melting the snow beneath the tent and generating condensation inside. For comfort you will want some kind of surface—a sleeping pad or wool blanket—underneath your sleeping bag to further separate your body from the cold snow.

Lean-tos are another option for winter camping in both the Adirondacks and Catskills. These are open shelters—imagine a small log cabin with a wall missing. They provide a ready-made shelter for day hikers and campers alike, and they are available on a first-come basis. They are built to accommodate six to eight people, and smaller groups cannot claim exclusive occupancy. Therefore, a group of three campers using a lean-to must leave space for as many as five other people. Sharing lean-tos is a common occurrence in the Adirondack High Peaks region, but much less so elsewhere. Mice, porcupines, and other critters also find lean-tos attractive. Even if a lean-to is your destination, always carry a tent just in case.

Melting snow is not the best method to obtain drinking water, but it does work in a pinch. Otherwise, look for a small, unfrozen stream to draw water from, or a hole in the ice of a larger stream. At higher elevations, where streams are much more likely to be completely frozen, running water can be a very scarce commodity. Always bring water to a full boil for two minutes before using it for consumption to protect yourself against giardiasis.

Lastly, let me make a case *against* the use of campfires. While it may sound counterintuitive not to have a fire to accompany you through the long, cold night, my experience has been that the excessive heat given off by one will only make the cold air *seem* that much colder. If you have brought all the right gear and clothing, you will stay warm quite nicely on your own. Note that in the Adirondack High Peaks, fires have been banned at all times of the year due to the limited amount of downed wood.

USING THIS BOOK

This guidebook is intended to be a trip-planning tool to help you identify winter hikes suited to your interests and abilities. Rather than being a list of the "best" hikes in the Adirondacks and Catskills, the sixty-five snowshoe routes listed herein offer a wide variety of hikes, from easy excursions leading to scenic lakes and Great Camps, to a multi-day trek up the tallest mountain in the state.

Therefore, to help you use this book to the best advantage, the description of each route is preceded by the following information:

Difficulty Ratings

The following are the considerations I used when rating the various routes:

Easy: These are trails that can be hiked by novice snowshoers, including families with young children, who have only summer hiking experience. These outings are short (no more than 4 miles round-trip) with minor elevation changes. They can include hikes to small mountains, secluded ponds, and historic Great Camps. The few obstacles included on these routes will give snowshoers a flavor of conditions found on harder hikes, without actually being a challenging ordeal.

Moderate: This rating covers a wide variety of trips, such as otherwise easy hikes that are greater than 4 miles in length round-trip, hikes with a greater overall elevation change, trails that are not always in tip-top maintenance, and hikes with situations that may require judgment on the part of the trip leader. These hikes do not automatically exclude novice snowshoers—experienced summer hikers, properly outfitted for winter, looking for a longer day in the woods, will find a moderate hike to their liking. At the same time, experienced snowshoers will also find much to hold their interest on these outings.

Difficult: While not requiring feats of superhuman endurance and ability, difficult hikes nevertheless are for snowshoers who have plenty of winter experience. These hikes include mountains with steep slopes—which can often be harder going down than up—or any hike where a pond or lake crossing is a recommended part of the route. This rating also includes poorly marked and maintained trails, or in some cases trails in remote, seldom-visited areas. A trail is therefore not always rated difficult because of its length or elevation change, but rather because of certain challenging conditions that may be encountered along the route.

Most Difficult: Anyone setting out on one of these outings must be prepared for the unexpected and be an expert at map-and-compass use. These routes include hikes to alpine summits, where fog or wind-blown snow can obscure even the most obvious trail, and hikes involving no established trails at all. The potential for demanding but rewarding winter hikes in the Catskills and Adirondacks is boundless, but only a few are included in this guide. They will give the reader an idea of the full range of wilderness snowshoeing available in New York State.

Round Trip

This is a simple statement of the total length of the snowshoe route, from the trailhead to the destination and back again. In the case of off-trail hikes, the distance may be listed as "variable" or as "minimum." A variable distance reflects the fact that there is no set distance to the hike, such as a hike with a number of potential destinations, which the snowshoer may or may not elect to see. A minimum distance reflects that portion of the hike that follows an access trail to reach the point where a bushwhack begins.

Hiking Time

This reflects the *minimum* amount of hiking time you should allow for the round-trip hike. The times given assume a pace of 2 miles per hour, although a number of factors may conspire to slow you down. The most likely culprit will be the condition of the snow itself, which can vary greatly from week to week. A deep, fresh

Enjoying the view of Wallface from Henderson Lake

snow can be as cumbersome as soft, thawing snow. Times may be listed as "variable" or "minimum" for the same reasons stated for round-trip distances.

Starting Elevation and Highest Point

This information provides the range of elevation you can expect to cover along the snowshoe route. The starting elevation is always that of the trailhead, but note that the highest point along the route is not always the endpoint. A route may have many minor ups and downs along the way, but if there are any problematic slopes it will certainly be noted in the text.

Maps

The Adirondack and Catskill regions are covered by dozens of U.S. Geological Survey (USGS) topographic maps, which remain the best source of detailed information. I have listed the quadrangle names for all of the USGS maps that cover the various snowshoe routes, to help you identify which ones you will need to carry in the woods.

What has changed dramatically in recent years, however, is how those maps are being disseminated to the public. While retailers still sell the printed maps, many people now use the Internet to obtain only the portions of the USGS maps they need. A number of websites allow users to download map images for free, most of them based on digitized images of the original USGS quads.

For a fee, Internet users can obtain larger, more durable copies of maps. One site called *www.mytopo.com* allows users to center their own topographic maps, joining adjacent quads to create a map useful for their own needs. The finished product is printed on a paper more durable than the USGS maps upon which they are based.

There are also several commercial maps available. National Geographic's *Trails Illustrated* series covers the entire Adirondack Park, and the New York–New Jersey Trail Conference publishes a similar series of maps of the Catskill Park. In both cases the maps show all marked trails, state land boundaries, and lean-tos, as well as topographic information; and in both cases, the maps are printed at a small scale. This makes them eminently useful in the trip-planning process.

Note that the maps provided in this book are for illustration and location purposes only, and they are by no means intended for in-the-field route finding.

Who to Contact

All of the public lands mentioned in this guide are managed by the State of New York. For each hike, I have listed the nearest regional office of the managing agency. If you require more current information about the area you plan to visit, refer to the appendix for the address and phone number.

Getting There

Each route will be preceded by detailed driving directions to the trailhead. These directions always begin from the nearest main highway or town, which should be easy to find using any standard road map. State highways are maintained in good condition throughout the winter. For references to byways and town roads, the best source of information is DeLorme's *New York State Atlas & Gazetteer*, which shows all of the routes mentioned. All of the directions refer to the following standard abbreviations: "I" for interstate highways, "US" for federal highways, "NY" for state highways, and "CR" for county routes.

A NOTE ABOUT SAFETY

Safety is an important concern in all outdoor activities. No guidebook can alert you to every hazard or anticipate the limitations of every reader. Therefore, the descriptions of roads, trails, routes, and natural features in this book are not representations that a particular place or excursion will be safe for your party. When you follow any of the routes described in this book, you assume responsibility for your own safety. Under normal conditions, such excursions require the usual attention to traffic, road and trail conditions, weather, terrain, the capabilities of your party, and other factors. Keeping informed on current conditions and exercising common sense are the keys to a safe, enjoyable outing.

The Mountaineers Books

Opposite: Pharaoh Mountain from Spectacle Pond

THE EASTERN ADIRONDACKS

A region as vast as the Adirondack Park could never be one homogenous whole. To many people, the Adirondack scenery can be summarized by saying "forest, rock, and water." Although this is essentially correct, the observant hiker will notice there are subtle variations on this theme as you travel from one corner of the park to another. Each region has its own signature that distinguishes it from every other part of the Adirondacks.

I have chosen to begin this book with the eastern Adirondacks, which because of the presence of Interstate 87—the Adirondack Northway—is the most accessible region. This highway makes it possible to shoot up into the park from the Albany area in just a few hours, and therefore the trails in this area are among the most popular. This region is also the most heavily developed portion of the park.

The Northway is not entirely to blame for that. Long before its construction in the 1960s, the eastern slopes of the Adirondack plateau were known to colonial explorers, armies, and settlers traveling between Lake Champlain and Lake George. Wars were fought here, and the European governments constructed a series of outposts at Crown Point, Ticonderoga, and the south end of Lake George.

For many generations, James Fenimore Cooper's *The Last of the Mohicans* was the epitome of wilderness adventure, although certain aspects of Hawkeye's woodcraft were probably as fictional as the character himself. Nevertheless, much of the action of the novel took place in this region, including the famous canoe chase across Lake George and the scenes in the Indian camp near Schroon Lake.

In the nineteenth century the Champlain valley was cleared for agriculture, and the mountainous interior was found to contain lucrative deposits of iron ore. With the additional effects of forest clearing for lumber and tanbark, this region had essentially lost its wilderness character by the time the Adirondack Park boundary was designated in 1892. The original park extended no further east than Schroon Lake, excluding all of the trails described in this chapter. However, in the first decades of the twentieth century, the state acquired several large tracts of these ex-industrial lands, including the Tongue Mountain Range and what is today the Pharaoh Lake Wilderness. The state included these areas in the Adirondack Park when they expanded the boundary in 1931.

The Pharaoh Lake Wilderness, which is the location of Hikes 1–5 in this guide, has a rich diversity of tempting destinations, from small ponds with descriptive, often original names, to rugged little hills scarred by glaciers and fires, to the larger mountains, Pharaoh and Treadway. It is no wonder, then, that this area deserves so much attention. The wealth of trails in this small wilderness makes it a delight for snowshoeing.

Since snowstorms tend to travel across the Adirondacks from west to east, the eastern region sees less accumulation than other localities. The slightly drier climate and lower elevations make this a region of pine, white birch, and oak, but this is anything but a "fringe" area. Mountains rise from the landscape in restless creativity, trapping ponds and lakes in the valleys between. A highly developed trail system reaches many of these places, with dozens of lean-tos to provide temporary shelter for winter hikers. This chapter will provide a sampling of the snowshoe routes available, although after tasting only a few of these outings you will agree that this is one of the most fun places to explore.

--1--
Goose Pond

Rating: Easy
Round trip: 3 miles
Hiking time: 1–2 hours
Starting elevation: 1000 feet
Highest point: 1200 feet
Map: USGS Pharaoh Mountain
Who to contact: NYS DEC Warrensburg Office

Getting there: The trailhead is easily accessible from the Northway (I-87) at Schroon Lake. From Exit 28, turn south on US 9 for 0.6 mile and bear left onto Alder Meadow Road. At 2.1 miles, bear left at a fork onto Crane Pond Road, which dead-ends 1.4 miles later at the trailhead parking area.

Goose Pond is a rather large body of water located in the northwestern corner of the Pharaoh Lake Wilderness. It is rimmed by beautiful white pine forests, and it lies at the foot of 2556-foot Pharaoh Mountain. The 1.5-mile route to the pond runs partly along an abandoned town road and partly along a narrow foot trail, but it passes entirely through coniferous forests of pine, hemlock, and spruce. It is an exceptionally handsome place for a short snowshoe hike.

The first 0.9 mile of the route to Goose Pond follows the continuing old road, which leads south from the parking area. It is a wide route that is easy to follow, with negligible grades—it is attractive to skiers and snowshoers alike. It takes about twenty minutes to reach the side trail to Goose Pond, which is marked by a small brown sign to the right of the road.

Leading south from the road, the trail quickly comes to a footbridge over the outlet of Alder Pond. It is a good bridge, but it is four feet above the water and only three feet wide—narrow enough to give pause to some hikers. Beyond, the trail climbs gradually through the hemlock-filled woods. The rich conifer forest provides a verdant canopy even on the bleakest winter day. After a forty-five-minute walk from your car, the trail ends near the northeastern corner of the pond. There is a large, degraded campsite here with a view of the pine-rimmed shoreline and Pharaoh Mountain rising like a pyramid beyond.

This short hike is really a great introduction to both snowshoeing and the Adirondacks in general. Allow about ninety minutes for the round-trip walk.

Pharaoh Mountain rises over Goose Pond.

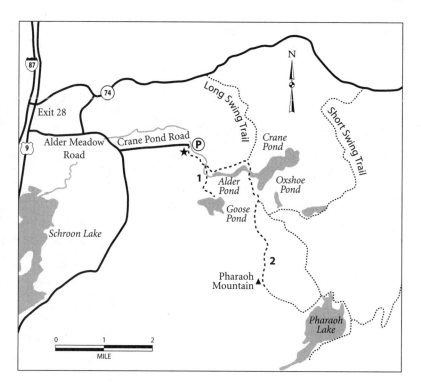

--2--

Pharaoh Mountain

Rating: Difficult
Round trip: 9.4 miles
Hiking time: 6 hours
Starting elevation: 1000 feet
Highest point: 2556 feet
Map: USGS Pharaoh Mountain
Who to contact: NYS DEC Warrensburg Office

Getting there: The trailhead is easily accessible from the Northway (I-87) at Schroon Lake. From Exit 28, turn south on US 9 for 0.6 mile and bear left onto Alder Meadow Road. At 2.1 miles, bear left at a fork onto Crane Pond Road, which dead-ends 1.4 miles later at the trailhead parking area.

View of the High Peaks from Pharaoh Mountain

Pharaoh Mountain, with an elevation of 2556 feet, is the tallest point in the Pharaoh Lake Wilderness, and its distinct profile is a landmark from nearly every hike in the region—including Hikes 1–5 in this guide. Dramatic cliffs mark the southern and southwestern slopes, while from the north and northeast the mountain almost appears to be a volcanic cone. The views from its bare summit encompass ponds and mountains in nearly every direction.

A winter ascent of Pharaoh Mountain does present a few special challenges, including the potential for strong, chilling winds at the summit. Nevertheless, winter climbers routinely make the ascent on snowshoes, and Pharaoh is certainly a good but strenuous winter climb.

This trip begins the same as Hike 1. The route to Pharaoh Mountain follows the entirety of the 1.9-mile abandoned continuation of the road to Crane Pond. Along the way you pass Alder Pond, above which you have your first glimpse of Pharaoh Mountain. At Crane Pond, bear right (south) on the red-marked foot trail, which crosses the outlet on a narrow bridge. A shady stretch of trail leads to an intersection at 2.6 miles. The mountain trail is the right fork, also marked with red.

The climbing begins a quarter mile later, gently at first, and much more steeply after the 3-mile mark, or an hour after Crane Pond. The forest cover makes a transition from second-growth hardwoods to spruce and fir, and then to scrub stands of conifer and birch near the summit. These offer scant protection from the wind. The end of the trail is a scramble, climbing 200 feet of elevation in just 200 yards.

The mountain has twin summits, divided by a slight cleft. The southern (right) knob offers the best view. Most of Pharaoh Lake is in view at the foot of the mountain, but surprisingly little of Schroon Lake is visible. Many of the High Peaks are visible to the north and northwest, and the Green Mountains of Vermont distinguish the eastern horizon. In addition, you should be able to identify Crane, Gore, and Snowy mountains in the central core of the park.

A trail continues down the southeast side of the mountain to Pharaoh Lake, for those few who are interested in making the loop trip. This trail to Pharaoh Lake is exceedingly steep in places, however.

-- 3 --
Short Swing Trail

Rating: Moderate
Round trip: 11.2 miles
Hiking time: 2 days
Starting elevation: 950 feet
Highest point: 1480 feet
Map: USGS Pharaoh Mountain, Graphite, and Eagle Lake
Who to contact: NYS DEC Warrensburg Office

Getting there: The trailhead is located on NY 74, some 8 miles east of Northway Exit 28 in Schroon Lake, or just 0.5 mile past the Ticonderoga town line.

One of the primary accesses into the lake-studded Pharaoh Lake Wilderness is called the Short Swing Trail (which, logically, is shorter than the Long Swing Trail, which traverses the backcountry from NY 74 to Putnam Pond). As a snowshoe route, it is a beauty. Officially, it is 5.5 miles long and ends near Oxshoe Pond, but it connects with other trails and passes so many potential bushwhacks that it is hard to confine your explorations just to the trail itself.

It passes six ponds, three lean-tos, and five small mountains with good views. Even if you stay the weekend, you will not likely get to see it all. This route will beckon you more than once.

The trail begins parallel to NY 74, crosses the outlet of Eagle Lake on a good bridge, follows an old roadbed between a conifer swamp and Ragged Mountain for a mile, and then bears left to climb at a gentle grade to a notch filled with tall white pines. A long descent leads to the Tubmill Marsh Lean-to at 2.3 miles, and then to a stream crossing at 2.5 miles.

Honey Pond is a small teardrop of ice that you pass at 2.9 miles. There is a short interlude through the woods, and then you reach Lilypad Pond, which is almost identical in size and shape to Honey. Its lean-to sits in a beautiful spot under a canopy of red pine, located just 0.1 mile along a red-marked trail that bears left at 3.4 miles.

The Short Swing Trail, marked in blue, bears right to climb to another saddle. It then descends along a rocky spine towards Horseshoe and Crab ponds, with views of Pharaoh Mountain developing through the trees. There are a few steep descents in this section, including a few rock ledges that may leave you wondering where to place your snowshoes as you step down. Both of the ponds have excellent potential for tent camping.

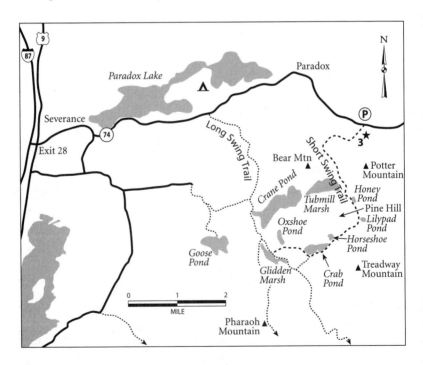

Lilypad Pond Lean-to

The trail follows the southern shore of Crab, although it is much more scenic to walk straight across the ice. From Crab's outlet, the trail descends again to Oxshoe, which also has a lean-to situated in a grove of red pine. The Short Swing Trail officially ends at 5.5 miles near Glidden Marsh, on the Long Swing Trail.

When exploring this area, leave your itinerary wide open. You may be able to spot a car at Crane Pond Road for a through trip, or you may make a big loop by returning across Crane Pond and Tubmill Marsh. The cliffs on Ragged Mountain, Potter Mountain, Peaked Hill, and Pine Hill are plainly visible from several points along the trail, and together with Bear Mountain any one of them would be a good side trip. It is a wanderer's delight!

--*4*--
Pharaoh Lake from the South

Rating: Moderate
Round trip: 7.2 miles
Hiking time: 3–4 hours
Starting elevation: 930 feet
Highest point: 1160 feet
Map: USGS Pharaoh Mountain
Who to contact: NYS DEC Warrensburg Office

Getting there: From Northway Exit 25 in Brant Lake, drive east on NY 8 for about 8 miles to Palisade Road. Follow Palisade Road for 1.6 miles to Beaver Pond Road, a right turn, and follow that to Pharaoh Road, which

Trail near Pharaoh Lake

is another right turn at 1.5 miles. Plowing ends on this narrow road at 0.4 mile, where there is limited winter parking.

The southern approach to Pharaoh Lake is one of the most popular, and it is probably best suited as a winter route because of flooding at Mill Brook. The route follows an old road and is considered a classic ski tour, but that does not make it a bore for snowshoers! This is a very pleasant woods walk, with attractive views along the way and an interesting destination at the end. Pharaoh Lake is one of the largest lakes entirely in the Forest Preserve, and it is home to six lean-tos. Note, however, that the statistics given in the information block above are for the walk to the lake's outlet, and they do not include the added distance for venturing across or around the lake itself.

The yellow-marked trail leads north through the notch between No. 8 and Park mountains, and enters a pine plantation just before reaching Mill Brook at 1.1 miles. This wide stream routinely floods its boggy banks, but there is a bridge and, assuming that the bog is frozen, most winter visitors get across much easier than their summer counterparts. The trail then angles northeast across the county line, which is marked by a stone monument that has become very hard to read. At 2.25 miles you reach a footbridge over Pharaoh Lake Brook. However, before crossing that bridge be sure to step off the trail to the left. From a wetland just upstream, there is a very good view of the cliffs on Pharaoh Mountain, which is one of the highlights of the entire hike. The mountain appears as though a large portion of its shoulder was severed and removed, exposing the tall rock face.

After crossing the bridge the trail pulls away from the outlet, passing along a subtle forest boundary: hardwoods upslope on the right, and a mixed-woods basin on the left. The trail then rejoins the stream just before reaching the lake.

An overgrown clearing across the stream was the site of an old logging camp. A smaller clearing on this side of the outlet, near the lake's small dam, was once the site of a ranger cabin.

This end of Pharaoh Lake is a long, narrow channel—the main body is further north. The trail forks beside the small dam, and these trails completely encircle the lake. Four of the six lean-tos are located near this southern end of the lake—two on either shore. A fifth is located on the eastern shore and the sixth is located on the northernmost bay at the far end of the lake. Pharaoh is a great place for a winter overnight, with the potential for a number of very good side trips.

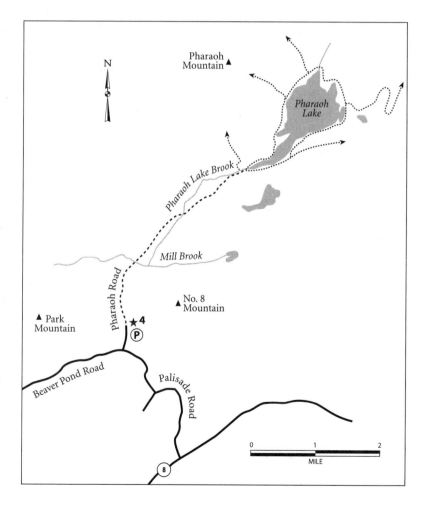

--*5*--
Spectacle Pond

Rating: Easy
Round trip: 3.4 miles
Hiking time: 1–2 hours
Starting elevation: 880 feet
Highest point: 1160 feet
Map: USGS Pharaoh Mountain
Who to contact: NYS DEC Warrensburg Office

Getting there: From the Northway (I-87), take Exit 28 in Schroon Lake and turn south on US 9 for 0.6 mile. Bear left onto Alder Meadow Road,

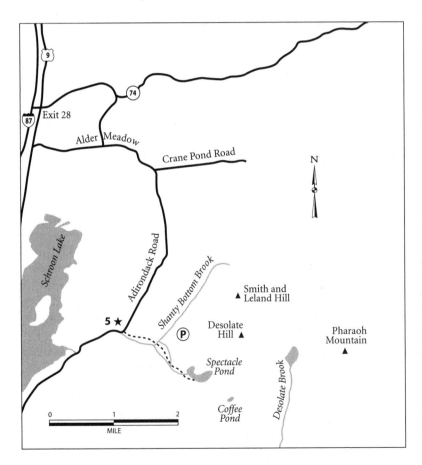

Pharaoh Mountain from Spectacle Pond

and at 2.1 miles bear right at a fork. This is Adirondack Road, which is shown as East Shore Road on some maps. (It is also called Redwing Road if you are approaching from the south.) Follow it south for 2.7 miles to the start of the trail, on the left side. There is no parking area, but there is room to park on the shoulder of this low-traffic road.

Like Goose Pond to the north (Hike 1), Spectacle Pond offers another easy hike to a secluded body of water seemingly at the foot of Pharaoh Mountain. However, from this angle the mountain takes on a strikingly different personality: instead of the cone with gentle slopes that you see from Goose, the mountain from Spectacle is a truncated massif with imposing cliffs. While

Spectacle Pond would be a pleasant destination in itself even without this view, this is definitely a hike you want to save for a day with good visibility.

The 1.7-mile trail presents and easy walk alongside the outlet of the pond, which you cross several times on small bridges. Hemlocks are found along most of the route, providing a verdant canopy to filter the sunlight. The route climbs 280 feet from the road to the pond, but the grades are minor. It is really a pleasant woods walk.

You cut left around a beaver meadow on the outlet, and just beyond, at 1.3 miles, you reach the boggy western extension of Spectacle Pond. This also marks the best place to view the ragged cliffs on Pharaoh Mountain, for from this end the pond is aligned directly with the mountain. The trail continues around the pond's south shore, crossing its outlet on a narrow log bridge and ending at a rocky little promontory on the pond's eastern lobe at 1.7 miles. The mountain is also visible from this end, but now the view of the cliffs is blocked by a nearby ridge. Nevertheless, the rocks make the perfect place for a lunch stop.

It takes about forty minutes to walk to the end of the trail. Snowshoers looking for a longer day in the woods will find a number of interesting bushwhack potentials in this area, the most promising of which might be a loop to Desolate Brook and Coffee Pond.

--6--
Fifth Peak

Rating: Moderate
Round trip: 5.4 miles
Hiking time: 3 hours
Starting elevation: 400 feet
Highest point: 1813 feet
Map: USGS Shelving Rock and Silver Bay
Who to contact: NYS DEC Warrensburg Office

Getting there: The beginning of the trail is called the Clay Meadow Trailhead. It is located on NY 9N, about 5 miles north of Bolton Landing. A brown DEC sign marks the start of the trail, but the parking area is 100 feet further north, beside an old pond-filled quarry.

The Tongue Mountain Range, which juts several miles into Lake George and divides its Northwest Bay from the main lake, is one of my favorite places to explore. Summer hikers enjoy a rugged trail that traverses the length of the

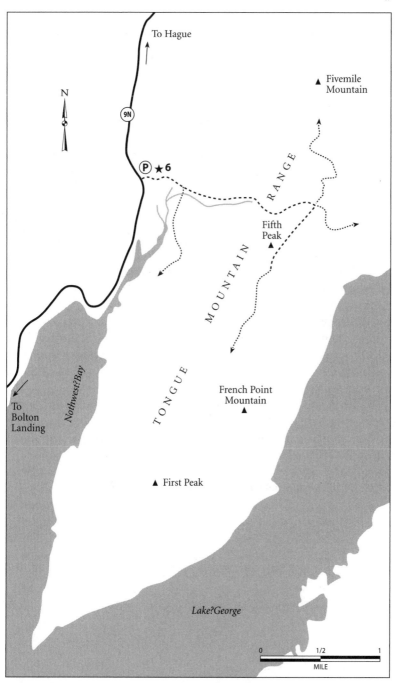

range, but in winter that trail would be very difficult on snowshoes. However, the winding trail to the lean-to on the summit of Fifth Peak from Northwest Bay Brook is snowshoe-friendly, although the snow itself is not likely to be as deep as other mountain ranges in the Adirondack Park (because of the relatively low elevation of the area and the range's southern orientation, the snowshoe season arrives later and ends earlier).

The trail begins in a plantation of white pine, and then crosses a long footbridge across the marshes at the head of Northwest Bay. At 0.4 mile a side trail bears right towards Montcalm Point, or the "Point of Tongue." This is the return leg for the summer hikers making the long loop up and over the range. For the snowshoe hike, however, bear left on the red-marked trail, which promptly begins to climb.

The trail was constructed by the Civilian Conservation Corps, and it bears a telltale wide grade and several switchbacks. Trailblazers in New York have long been resisting the concept of the switchback, which is a zigzagging route that is intended to avoid the steepest slopes. Most Adirondack trails take the most direct route straight up the mountain, and so the switchbacks on this trail, however subtle, seem daring in their originality. You may spot a small, stone retaining wall at one sharp left turn.

At 1.9 miles you reach the crest of the ridge and the trail that follows its length. Turn right and half a mile later bear left onto the yellow-marked spur trail that leads to the summit of Fifth Peak and its lean-to. In 2.7 miles you have climbed 1400 feet from your car.

The clearing is rimmed by a forest of red oak, with openings that permit views of the Lake George Narrows, a corner of Northwest Bay, and the parade of mountains that constitutes the southern reaches of the Tongue Range. Across the Narrows, Black Mountain rises as a cliff-scarred massif from the frozen lake. The lean-to makes this an attractive camping destination, but of course the only source of water on this summit is the snow itself.

Opposite: Hurricane Mountain from Lost Pond

KEENE VALLEY TO LAKE PLACID

The snowshoe routes in this chapter will acquaint you with one of the most scenic highway corridors in the Northeast: NY 73 from Northway (I-87) Exit 30 into Lake Placid, the two-time host village of the Winter Olympics. Along the way the road travels through Chapel Pond Pass and the Cascade Lakes Pass, where ice-bound cliffs rise above the highway. On any hospitable winter day, dozens of cars can be parked along the road in these passes as ice climbers pursue their sport.

Being hemmed in by mountains on nearly all sides, the communities of Keene, Keene Valley, and Lake Placid all thrive on an economy based on outdoor recreation. Furthermore, nearly all of the state land surrounding these valleys is protected in a motorless condition, with no fewer than six wilderness areas and one primitive area in the immediate vicinity. The snowshoeing and cross-country skiing possibilities are boundless.

The primary draw for hikers in all seasons is the High Peaks, which will be described in the next chapter. With a few exceptions, those mountains are clustered south and west of NY 73. However, the mountains that lie across the road, while not rising above 4000 feet, are no less impressive, and the views from their summits are no less attractive.

Some of these, such as the Sentinel Range, are truly trackless and wild. The Soda Range (more colorfully known as Nun-da-ga-o Ridge) features a long, open ridgeline with sweeping views into the High Peaks, but near-vertical pitches and snow-laden trees make this route a real challenge in winter. It is so difficult that few people attempt it outside of the summer and fall months.

The following three snowshoe routes, however, are a sample of the region's best winter hikes. They will get you started in this region, and they make a good primer in winter hiking before you tackle the larger, less forgiving High Peaks.

Lake Placid hosted the Olympics in 1932 and 1980, but as you drive through town you may think the games never ended. All of the venues have been retained and even kept up-to-date, including the bobsled run, the ski jumps, and the downhill ski runs on Whiteface. Lake Placid was the last small village to host the Olympics, which have since grown too large for a town of this size to handle on its own. There is perennial talk of bringing the winter games back a third time, perhaps in a joint bid with Montreal or in a regional bid involving the entire Adirondack area.

--7--

Lost Pond and Weston Mountain

Rating: Moderate to Lost Pond, difficult to Weston Mountain
Round trip: 4.8 miles
Hiking time: 4 hours
Starting elevation: 2132 feet
Highest point: 3182 feet
Map: USGS Lewis
Who to contact: NYS DEC Ray Brook Office

Getting there: To find the trailhead, turn onto Hurricane Road (CR 13) in the village of Keene, just south of the NY 9N/73 fork. Follow it uphill for 2.2 miles to O'Toole Road, which bears left just as Hurricane Road hooks sharply right. O'Toole Road is a narrow, winding town road, and winter maintenance ends at 0.9 mile. Because the snowplows need to

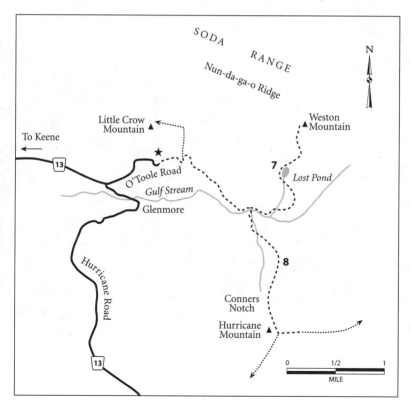

turn around here, there is room for only a small number of cars to park. Thus, either arrive early or be flexible in your plans.

The town of Keene is a hikers' haven. It seems as though every highway and back road leads to a mountain trailhead. Thousands of hikers flock to the High Peaks to the west of Keene Valley, and in winter they literally have to be bussed to one unplowed trailhead. To the east, the somewhat smaller mountains are nearly as popular for their views *of* the High Peaks. Skiers enjoy the wide trails that trace the valleys and notches, but the mountain climbs are largely the realm of the snowshoers.

Hurricane Mountain from Lost Pond

Tucked away in this mountainous region are a handful of small tarns rimmed with snow-laden spruces and firs. Lost Pond, nestled on a shoulder of Weston Mountain in the Hurricane Mountain Primitive Area, is as beautiful and secluded as any that you will find. Easily reached by a well-maintained trail, the pond is also the site of an attractive lean-to. The view from the north end of the pond across to Hurricane Mountain is outstanding.

The trail continues beyond the lean-to to the summit of Weston Mountain, which expands the view to include the High Peaks beyond Keene Valley. Light trail maintenance and several very steep pitches earned this part of the trail a difficult rating.

From the winter trailhead, follow the unplowed road into state land to the summer trailhead, which was once a small homestead (an island of trees covers the stone-lined cellar hole). At just below 2250 feet, this has the distinction of being the second highest trailhead in the Adirondacks, after another trailhead a hundred feet higher in the Stephenson Range near Wilmington.

The trail begins to the right, crossing a narrow footbridge. The first 1.1 miles follow an old roadbed through the birch-filled woods, and the walking is very easy. About forty minutes from your car, you reach the Gulf Brook Lean-to, where the trail to Hurricane Mountain (Hike 8) bears right.

Bear left at the lean-to for the trail to Lost Pond. You parallel Gulf Brook a short distance and then cross the frozen outlet stream of the pond. Shortly beyond, the trail makes a sharp bend left, beginning the 0.6-mile climb to the level of the pond. Dense forest cover prevents any views until you cross the outlet a second time and reach the short side path leading to the foot of the pond. Weston Mountain rises above.

As the trail continues to the north end, look back for the view to Hurricane. The Biesemeyer Lean-to is hidden in the woods nearby, the perfect shelter for a winter camping trip—if you are prepared for the colder temperatures that attend a pond at this elevation, which tops 2800 feet. You reach this spot about ninety minutes from the start.

The continuing trail leads north to Weston Mountain, ascending two steep defiles in the rock before topping out on the summit, with its grand view back across the terrain you have just covered. The short but difficult climb takes a half hour or more.

Maps show the trail continuing as a loop along the Soda Range to Big Crow Mountain. This is the Nun-da-ga-o Ridge Trail—one of the most beautiful summer hikes in the Adirondacks, but nearly impassable in winter. This one should be left to the experts.

-- 𝒈 --

Hurricane Mountain

Rating: Moderate
Round trip: 5.6 miles
Hiking time: 3 hours
Starting elevation: 2132 feet
Highest point: 3678 feet
Map: USGS Lewis and Keene Valley
Who to contact: NYS DEC Ray Brook Office

Getting there: To find the trailhead, turn onto Hurricane Road (CR 13) in the village of Keene, just south of the NY 9N/73 fork. Follow it uphill for 2.2 miles to O'Toole Road, which bears left just as Hurricane Road hooks sharply right. O'Toole Road is a narrow, winding town road, and winter maintenance ends at 0.9 mile. Because the snowplows need to turn around here, there is room for only a small number of cars to park. Thus, either arrive early or be flexible in your plans.

For such a large mountain, this route up the north face of Hurricane presents a very moderate climb. Except at the summit itself, there are no rocky ledges to scramble over, and only a few short steps along the trail that might be considered steep. Therefore, this route is perfectly suited to a wide variety of winter hikers, and the bald summit is definitely worth the climb. This was a fire tower mountain, too. The tower was still standing as of 2005, but it was scheduled to be relocated so that the mountain can be reclassified as a wilderness area.

The trail to Hurricane begins the same as described in Hike 7. Follow the first 1.1 miles of the trail to the Gulf Brook Lean-to. Indeed, either this shelter or the one at Lost Pond would make an excellent base camp for this winter ascent, if you wanted to extend your visit over an entire weekend.

Bear right at the intersection by the lean-to, crossing the frozen Gulf Brook and cutting around a knoll to another stream, this one the unnamed tributary that drains Conners Notch. The trail follows the stream to the mountain, crossing it a number of times. (Except at the beginning and end of winter, or during a mild winter, the brook should be solidly frozen. There are no bridges on this trail.)

The trail slowly rises beside the brook and then climbs more noticeably once it reaches the foot of the mountain. At one point it seems as though you are being led to Conners Notch. The forest consists almost exclusively of paper

Hoarfrost on Hurricane Mountain

birch, with its distinctive tassels of salmon-colored bark peeling off of the trees. The grade is never more than moderately steep, even as you enter the spruce-fir zone just below the summit.

About an hour from the lean-to, you reach a shoulder high on the mountain where the trail from NY 9N comes up on the right. The summit is straight ahead, and here is the one scramble you will encounter. Winds usually sweep the summit free of snow. There are views in all directions. Although Hurricane is not a High Peak itself, it nevertheless keeps close company with them. Giant is the closest, just on the other side of NY 9N to the south, but across Keene Valley is a wide and gratuitous display of other peaks: Dix, the Wolf Jaws (Hike 10), Marcy (Hike 12), Big Slide, and Porter, to name some of the most distinct. To the north is Lost Pond and Weston Mountain, and beyond them is the very rugged Jay Range.

--*9*--

Haystack Mountain

Rating: Difficult
Round trip: 6.6 miles
Hiking time: 4–5 hours
Starting elevation: 1640 feet
Highest point: 2880 feet
Map: USGS Saranac Lake
Who to contact: NYS DEC Ray Brook Office

Getting there: The trailhead is located at the north end of a wide turnout on NY 86 midway between Ray Brook and Lake Placid. It would be difficult to miss.

What makes this a difficult hike is the steep final pitch to the summit, as well as a handful of stream crossings that could be an obstacle if not fully frozen. Beyond that, this 3.3-mile hike to a modest-sized mountain west of Lake Placid

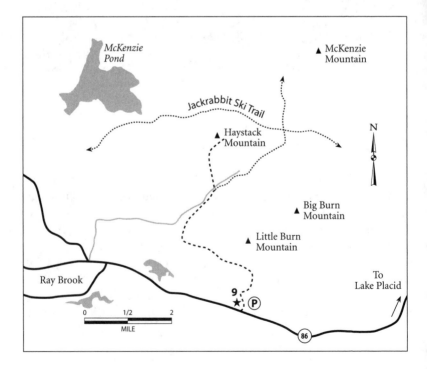

View toward the High Peaks from Haystack Mountain

is a great climb through birch-filled woods, with a view from the top that takes in much of the High Peaks region in one sweeping vista.

The trailhead is the primary entrance into the McKenzie Mountain Wilderness. Marked with blue disks, the trail begins in a plantation of white pine and Norway spruce, leading northerly and even northeast before finally swinging west towards its destination. It traverses the lower slopes of Little Burn Mountain through a forest of paper birch, aspen, and red maple—sure signs that a fire did, in fact, sweep this mountainside. On a gray winter day, the whites of the birches, the graphite gray of the full-sized aspens, and the snow all around can make the woods appear perfectly colorless.

You gain some elevation on Little Burn, but lose it all as the trail bears downhill towards Little Ray Brook. The trail intercepts an old roadway at 1.5 miles, forty-five minutes from the start, and then begins to climb in earnest beside the brook, following it northeast. After passing a set of concrete foundations on the right and an icy gorge on the left, the trail forks.

Bear left for Haystack, soon coming to the crossing of Little Ray Brook below a concrete dam (an abandoned municipal water source). Now you begin to climb! The several steep pitches alternate with level terraces, until finally you are presented with the final scramble up the side of the summit knob. The trail is only slightly less steep than the surrounding rock walls, but with the careful use of your ski poles and built-in crampons, you will find yourself on top in a matter of minutes. The last few minutes to the summit proper are comparatively mild.

From the broad, snowy clearing on top, the vista extends from the Sentinel Range across Lake Placid, to the Saranac Lake region to the west. Among the prominent High Peaks in view are Marcy, Algonquin, and the Seward Range. In the near distance the cluster of buildings surrounded by an oversized clearing is the former athletes' village from the 1980 Winter Games. Though difficult to discern from this angle, each one resembles the five Olympic rings. The facility now serves as a prison.

Opposite: On the summit of Lower Wolf Jaw

THE EASTERN HIGH PEAKS WILDERNESS

One of the paradoxes of legally designated wilderness—where man is a visitor who does not remain—is that the moniker "wilderness" often makes these areas more appealing to hikers than other areas. However, the High Peaks Wilderness is one place that would be overwhelmingly popular no matter its legal designation. Containing the state's highest peak, Mount Marcy, and the majority of the other 4000-foot summits, the dramatic terrain is simply unrivaled by any other Adirondack region.

Well over 100,000 people descend upon this wilderness annually. There has been a corresponding decrease in the quality of the trails and campsites, prompting the DEC to take stringent management actions. Some of the relevant special regulations for visiting the High Peaks are outlined in the Introduction.

Winter may be the most enjoyable season to visit the High Peaks. Not only are the crowds reduced to tolerable numbers (but still much higher than you will encounter in any of the following chapters) but also the trails are in much better shape. Spring and summer erosion has taken a heavy toll on many High Peaks trails, but in winter all of the valley trails are well-packed surfaces ideal for winter hiking. Unless you plan to bushwhack, you will rarely have to break trail yourself.

As popular and well known as the High Peaks are today, they remained unknown and unscaled for a surprisingly long time. The first recorded ascent of Mount Marcy did not occur until 1837, thirty years after the Lewis and Clark expedition. The mountain was given two names that year: the survey party that climbed it named it after the governor who organized their expedition, and the writer C. F. Hoffman bestowed the more romantic name Tahawus, a purported Indian word meaning "cloud-splitter." Marcy was the name that stuck, although the name Tahawus has never been forgotten.

Later in the nineteenth century, guides began to blaze trails to the tops of the more scenic peaks, but it was not until 1921 that someone began to consider all of the highest peaks together. This was Robert Marshall, his brother George, and their family guide Herbert Clark. Using the first generation of USGS topological quadrangles, they identified forty-two separate peaks exceeding 4000 feet in elevation, and then proceeded to climb all of them in one summer, using the Marshall family camp on Lower Saranac Lake as a base. Eight of these were first ascents. Sometime later, the Marshall brothers realized there were four additional peaks that met their criteria, and which they had overlooked previously. They promptly returned to climb those as well.

Even though modern maps have proven there are really only forty-two High Peaks, the feat of climbing the forty-six that the Marshall brothers counted remains engrained in Adirondack hiking culture to this day. Indeed, as you snowshoe these mountain trails you will repeatedly meet people who will ask you, "So, are you working on your forty-six?" You rarely meet anyone who answers no, or who has not already made all of their ascents. The devotion to the peaks can be so strong among some hikers that they forget that this region accounts for only a small percent of the total acreage of the Adirondack Park.

Snowshoeing in the High Peaks presents special challenges because weather extremes are more likely to be encountered. What begins as a balmy day in the foothills can prove to be quite blustery on the summits, and whiteouts can reduce visibility to zero. The importance of dressing in layers, watching the weather, and keeping track of your location has never been more important than it is here. In addition, most High Peaks trips tend to be long. Because of all of these factors, four of the following five snowshoe routes have earned difficult and most difficult ratings. These are not hikes to be taken lightly.

--10--
Lower Wolf Jaw

Rating: Most Difficult
Round trip: 10.4 miles
Hiking time: 8 hours
Starting elevation: 1280 feet
Highest point: 4173 feet
Map: USGS Keene Valley
Who to contact: NYS DEC Ray Brook Office

Getting there: Public parking is accommodated at one of either two parking areas at the southern intersection of NY 73 with Ausable Road, south of Keene Valley, and roughly 7 miles northwest of Northway Exit 30. Both lots tend to fill up early on weekends, and there is no parking elsewhere.

The Adirondack High Peaks remain difficult mountains to climb because of their wilderness status. Most remain very remote, requiring long walks just to reach their bases, and many hikers end their trips by walking out of the woods by flashlight. Even those peaks nearest the roads are deceptively difficult, and this is especially the case with Lower Wolf Jaw, the northernmost and least secluded summit in the Great Range.

The Great Range is a place of outstanding beauty and difficult hiking. In addition to the Wolf Jaws, it includes Armstrong, Gothics, Basin, and

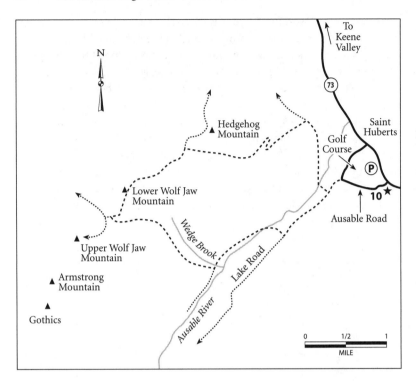

Saddleback; for sentimental reasons, Mount Marcy is usually regarded as the end cap of the range, although it is not completely in alignment with the others. Many hikers rank Gothics among their most favorite Adirondack mountains, but its bare rock slopes make it a real challenge in winter. The Wolf Jaws are so named because of the deep col that divides them: from a distance, the two peaks resemble the open jaws of a wolf.

This long and difficult loop ascends Lower Wolf Jaw by way of the Wedge Brook Trail, and descends via the W. A. White Trail. It begins and ends at the Ausable Club, a nineteenth century resort that is still in operation, and one that permits public access to their property. In fact, the club once owned many of the surrounding peaks, including the Great Range, before conveying them to the state-owned Forest Preserve. Public access across the remaining private land is free, but it is restricted to marked trails. There is no camping until you reach state land, and the club quite emphatically forbids pets.

The hike begins by walking up Ausable Road for about 0.4 mile from the NY 73 parking areas to the golf course, and then bearing left onto Lake Road. Register at the guard station and then proceed through the elaborate gate.

The Lake Road is not plowed, but it is nevertheless a well-traveled, hard-packed thoroughfare. You may not need snowshoes until about a mile later, where you bear right onto a foot trail for Canyon Bridge. This link trail leads across Gill Brook to the Ausable River, and then to a steep scramble up to the West River Trail, where you should bear left. This highly scenic route leads high above the river with mountain views already developing, including the rather jarring burned area on Noonmark Mountain. At 3.1 miles, next to a frozen waterfall and its splash pool, bear right on the Wedge Brook Trail.

The trail promptly begins to climb steeply. Ninety minutes from the start, you finally reach state land. The trail leads to a level area below massive slides on Lower Wolf Jaw, swings west, and then really begins to climb. The going can be very slow—this is a very steep section of trail. At a marked intersection on the side of the mountain, the right fork is the direct route to the mountain. I recommend the left fork, however, which is only 0.2 mile longer but much more scenic. It takes you into Wolf Jaws Col first, where you can appreciate the slide on the upper peak before angling right to climb Lower Wolf Jaw at the next intersection.

Either way, the scramble up to the summit is even steeper than below. Allow for at least three and a half hours to reach the summit. Although it is

Dix, Dial, and Nippletop from the summit of Lower Wolf Jaw

wooded, there are very good views in several directions, including one east-ward to Giant and Dix, with the Green Mountains on the horizon. Equally good is the view across Johns Brook Valley to Klondike, Yard, and Algonquin. This view gives one a particularly good sense for the breadth of the High Peaks Wilderness and the amount of country waiting to be explored. You can also see down the string of peaks constituting the Great Range, with Marcy presiding over the head of the Johns Brook Valley.

The descent along the W. A. White Trail northeast from the summit is hardly any easier than the ascent. There is a near-vertical chute as you leave the summit, and then as you traverse the knob known as the Wolf Chin you are briefly on a steep side-slope, with the Johns Brook Valley gaping below. Add to this the fact that the trail is not well marked and it becomes clear that this is a difficult trail, even as a descent.

Bear right at a series of intersections as you lose elevation, entering a forest that has been logged recently. The route eventually brings you to a long footbridge over the Ausable River, and just beyond is the guard station at the trailhead.

The return along the W. A. White trail seems to see so little winter use and is fraught with so many difficulties that if you are really skittish it would be much simpler—and probably faster—to simply return via Wedge Brook.

Some people who climb to Lower Wolf Jaw may also be tempted to "shoot up" to neighboring Upper Wolf Jaw while they are in the vicinity. If you fall under this category, bear in mind that the climb to the summit from the col is as steep as the climb to Lower Wolf Jaw, with a greater vertical rise. Climbing both peaks would turn an already difficult experience into a grueling slog through the snow.

--11--
Avalanche Pass

Rating: Moderate
Round trip: 9.2
Hiking time: 5 hours
Starting elevation: 2180 feet
Highest point: 2985 feet
Map: USGS Keene Valley
Who to contact: NYS DEC Ray Brook Office

Getting there: The trailhead is located on property owned by the Adirondack Mountain Club. It is open to the public, but the club does charge

Avalanche Pass from Lake Colden

a fee for parking. From NY 73 east of Lake Placid and the Olympic ski jump, turn south onto Adirondack Loj Road. The parking area is at the far end of the road, just to the left of the club's tollbooth. This is one of the largest, most developed trailheads in New York, including a hikers' building with restrooms and supplies. There is often a forest ranger present as well.

Most snowshoe trips into the heart of the High Peaks Wilderness are difficult treks at best, mostly because of the distances and terrain involved. However, here is one you can do as a moderate day trip, and it leads to one of the most spectacular mountain passes in the northeast. It is no surprise that this is also a very popular route, but in this case its popularity is an advantage: when trails elsewhere are impassable with a deep, fresh snow, this one is almost always packed down and in good shape.

Follow the blue-marked VanHoevenberg Trail from the east end of the parking area. There is little chance of getting lost on the 2.3-mile section leading to Marcy Dam, as this is *the* trunk trail from which every other trail begins. Marcy Dam impounds a tiny pond with a big view, and it is an extremely popular camping area. There is a ranger station near the dam.

Cross the dam and bear right around the pond, following the yellow-marked trail along Marcy Brook. This trail leads past several more lean-tos before climbing towards Avalanche Pass. Near the height-of-land, you reach the site of the most recent avalanche in the pass. This one was triggered in September 1999, when the remains of Hurricane Floyd brought a deluge to the mountains. The water saturated the soil, which was merely a thin covering

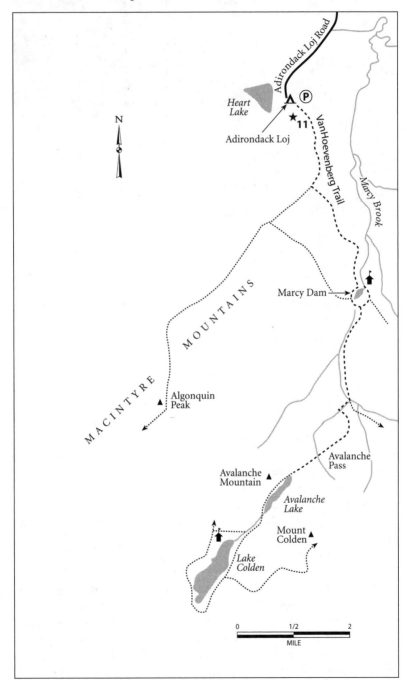

N

over the smooth bedrock. The landslide swept bare a broad swath on the side of Mount Colden, leaving a densely packed debris pile in the pass.

The trail cuts through the debris and then dodges several large boulders before reaching the north end of Avalanche Lake at 4.6 miles. The view of this frozen pool at the foot of the enormous rock face on Colden is unparalleled, and there can be no doubt how the lake got its name.

For a fulfilling hike, you do not need to go any further. However, most winter hikers continue across the lake to neighboring Lake Colden—which like Marcy Dam is a hub of activity in every season. It, too, boasts an interior ranger station.

Avalanche Pass has many stories to tell, but the one most often told is that of "Hitch Up Matilda." Matilda Fielding was a woman of good size who was making a multiday trek through the High Peaks in 1868 with her husband and niece. Their guide was Bill Nye. When they reached Avalanche Lake, the only way to walk through the pass involved using a rock ledge at the side of the lake that was several feet underwater. In order that his clients might stay dry, Nye offered to carry the three of them across. Matilda was the first one to venture onto Nye's back, but as she began to slip downward and ever closer to the water, her husband and niece called out from shore: "Hitch up, Matilda, *hitch up!*"

Nye's lively retelling of the story to Seneca Ray Stoddard inspired the name for the series of catwalks and bridges that now span that same troublesome section of the shore—the Hitch-up-Matildas. Hikers no longer have to bum a ride on somebody's back to traverse the pass.

--12--
Mount Marcy from Upper Works

Rating: Most Difficult
Round trip: 20.6 miles
Hiking time: 2 days
Starting elevation: 1772 feet
Highest point: 5344 feet
Map: USGS Mount Marcy, Ampersand Lake, Santanoni Peak, and Keene Valley
Who to contact: NYS DEC Ray Brook Office

Getting there: From Northway Exit 29 at North Hudson, drive west on the Blue Ridge Road for 17 miles to the right turn for Tahawus. Follow

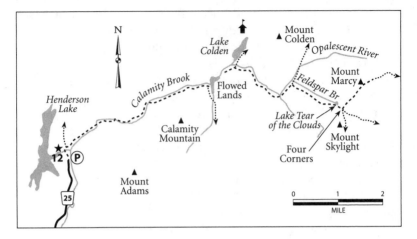

this road, CR 25, to a fork at 6.25 miles. Turn left and continue to the
Upper Works parking area at the end of the road, 9.9 miles from Blue
Ridge Road.

Mount Marcy is the tallest mountain in New York State, and because of its
remoteness, its ruggedness, and its alpine summit, it is a difficult winter climb.
Unlike most other Adirondack peaks, Marcy has a distinct tree line with a
summit that is completely exposed. Conditions can vary greatly between the
foot of the mountain and its top, where the weather can get quite blustery
without even trying very hard. If the visibility is poor for whatever reason, it
can be more than just an inconvenience—many winter hikers have lost their
way and descended the wrong side of the summit.

This is an excursion that is best done in a minimum of two days—allow
three days if you don't want to push yourself. There are lean-tos in abundance
along the route, especially around Flowed Lands and Lake Colden. The route
passes a number of well-known landmarks, and it is perhaps the most scenic
approach to the mountain. Beyond Lake Colden is an exceptionally beautiful
winter climb.

Follow the well-traveled trail north from the Upper Works trailhead, bear-
ing right at the first intersection. It is a 4.7-mile trek up through the Calamity
Brook drainage, gaining 1000 feet, and passing the stone monument at Calamity
Pond that marks the spot where David Henderson, one of the founders of the
Tahawus iron mine, was fatally shot in an accidental discharge of a pistol. The
trail ends at the edge of the Flowed Lands beside a pair of lean-tos.

The Flowed Lands are the site of a former reservoir on the Opalescent
River. When the dam breached in the 1970s, DEC allowed the site to revert to

its natural state as a wetland. In addition to the lean-tos near the trail, there are several more scattered around the shoreline. All of them are popular by virtue of their central location in the mountains.

Summer hikers are limited to the rough trail around this former lake, a trail that no one uses in winter. Instead, continue straight across the ice, reentering the woods at the far end on the south side of the Opalescent River. There is a very popular camping area here in the flats between Flowed Lands

The summit of Mount Marcy as viewed from treeline

and Lake Colden—be sure to abide by the DEC's signs and posted regulations. Lake Colden's shoreline is also dotted with scenic lean-tos.

From the dam at Lake Colden, follow the red-marked trail that bears right, southeast, to continue along the south side of the Opalescent. Some steep pitches arise as you ascend past a deep gorge known as the Flume. For a moment the trail is at the precipice of a deep and narrow chasm. In the secluded valley above, you will find lean-tos at Uphill and Feldspar brooks. Although not as busy as those near Lake Colden, there are few weekends when these shelters are not occupied.

At an intersection near Feldspar Brook, 2.3 miles from Lake Colden, bear right on the trail to Four Corners. Here is the longest, steepest part of the trip, with an ascent of 1027 feet in 1.6 miles. The worst climbing ends at Lake Tear of the Clouds, the highest pond source of the Hudson River, and the place where Vice President Theodore Roosevelt was camping the day he learned that President McKinley had been shot by an assassin. Camping is not permitted at this elevation.

From the Four Corners it is just 0.8 mile to Marcy's summit, a left turn. It is in this section that you climb out of the balsam forest into the alpine zone, where instead of a firm snowpack you may find drifts, icy ledges, and bare rock. To the southeast the mountainside drops nearly two thousand feet into Panther Gorge—this should be incentive enough for you to pick your way carefully during a whiteout!

The mountain is named for William Marcy, the state governor who assembled the team of scientists who would become the first people to reach the summit. For many decades the Adirondacks had gone without being surveyed, and little was known about the area at all. At one point it was believed that the Catskills contained the state's highest point. The legislature appropriated funds for a natural history survey in 1836, which would include an expedition into the mountains of northern New York to determine once and for all what was there.

Led by chief geologist Ebenezer Emmons, the expedition ventured into the High Peaks that year and camped at the lake they named Lake Colden. Poor weather delayed many of their plans, however, and although one member of the party spotted a peak that appeared to tower above the rest, it would not be until the following year that they would get the chance to climb it.

This time Emmons returned to the mountains with an expedition team of twelve that included both scientists and artists. Their route was very similar to the one described above. Their barometric readings confirmed that these mountains were indeed head and shoulders above the Catskills in terms of elevation. They reached the summit on August 5, 1837, and named it after the sitting state governor. They estimated its elevation to be 5300 feet.

In October of that same year, the *New York Mirror* ran an article by Charles Fenno Hoffman that suggested that the original Indian name for the mountain was Tahawus, or Cloud-Splitter. Marcy, however, was the name that stuck, although Tahawus and Cloud-Splitter are also mentioned on the commemorative plaque placed on the summit a century after the first ascent. Marcy, the mountain, remains the most charismatic of Adirondack climbs, although the memory of the man for which it was named has long since faded into obscurity.

--13--
Duck Hole via the Preston Ponds

Rating: Difficult
Round trip: 11 miles
Hiking time: 6–8 hours or 2 days
Starting elevation: 1772 feet
Highest point: 2180 feet
Map: USGS Ampersand Lake and Santanoni Peak
Who to contact: NYS DEC Ray Brook Office

Getting there: From Northway Exit 29 in North Hudson, drive west on the Blue Ridge Road for 17 miles to the right turn for Tahawus. Follow this road, CR 25, to a fork at 6.25 miles. Turn left and continue to the Upper Works parking area at the end of the road, 9.9 miles from Blue Ridge Road.

The recent acquisition of Henderson Lake and the Preston Ponds has opened up an outstanding winter trek, gaining in popularity among snowshoers and skiers alike. The public had always been allowed to hike through the pass to reach the Cold River valley, but now it is possible to leave the trail and walk across the ice, trimming 2 miles off the length of the hike. Doing so has also improved the scenic quality of the hike a hundredfold; the original trail kept to the woods and offered few glimpses of the lakes or the surrounding mountains. One of the highlights is the view through Indian Pass, dominated by the sheer cliffs of Wallface Mountain.

The hike begins at Henderson Lake, which is the official source of the Hudson River. It ends at Duck Hole, a remote pond enlarged by an old log dam at the head of the Cold River. The Cold River country is among the most remote of any area in the state, and this hike offers the best chance for snowshoers to get a taste of it. A lean-to on Henderson Lake and the two at Duck Hole offer shelter for backpackers seeking to extend this into a multiday excursion.

From the trailhead register at Upper Works, follow the well-traveled trunk trail north to the bridge over the fledgling Hudson at 0.3 mile and turn left. The old roadway ends shortly beyond at the large dam that creates Henderson Lake. Setting off across the ice, you will forget you are on a man-made impoundment as soon as you reach the main body of the lake. Follow it north, with MacNaughton and Wallface mountains looming above you. The latter

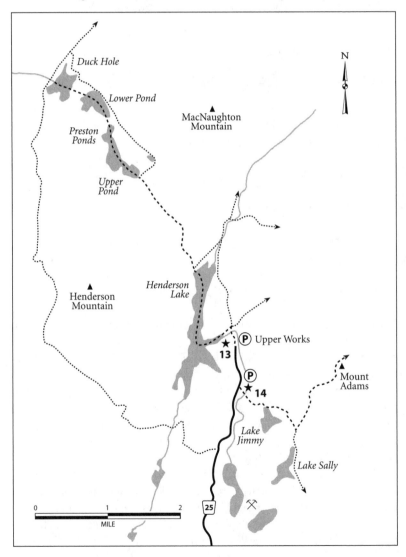

Hiking across Henderson Lake, Wallface Mountain in the distance

leads your eye to Indian Pass, which has been attracting explorers almost as long as there have been people in the Adirondacks. The shore of the lake is quite rugged, with many rock bluffs repeating the motif of the mountainous backdrop. Most of these bluffs are capped with cedar trees.

A prominent inlet stream near the northwest corner of the lake marks the point where you should leave the lake for the trail to the Preston Ponds. There is a lean-to set back in the woods, beside the trail. What follows is a 1.8-mile trek up through the valley, which narrows into a pass between Henderson and MacNaughton mountains. A short descent through the pass brings you to Upper Pond.

The hiking trail bears right here and continues climbing to Hunter Pond. You are done with the trail, so go straight to the big pond and keep going. Like Henderson Lake, Upper Pond has steep, cedar-lined shores. A long, uneven arm of Henderson Mountain cradles the pond to the west, with a tall set of cliffs in view. The steep slopes of MacNaughton seem to plunge into the pond to your right, with walls of colored ice coating the various ledges. As you proceed, the remote Sawtooth Range comes into view.

A short, unmarked path links the Upper and Lower ponds, and from the latter the Seward Range is also visible. To get to Duck Hole you will have to make a short bushwhack alongside the outlet. The lean-tos are both located next to the Duck Hole dam, near the site of a long-gone ranger station.

If you are backpacking to Duck Hole, you may be interested in varying your return route by following the trail south through the Santanoni-Henderson pass. The trail between Duck Hole and the pass is lightly used; it crosses an unnamed brook a number of times and climbs steeply to the pass. The Santanoni Lean-to sits at the height-of-land, and beyond the trail is well used by snowshoers accessing the Santanoni Range. Returning through this secluded valley adds to the difficulty of the hike and requires walking 1.6 miles of road back to the Upper Works trailhead.

--14--
Mount Adams

Rating: Difficult
Round trip: 4.6 miles
Hiking time: 3–4 hours
Starting elevation: 1772 feet
Highest point: 3520 feet
Map: USGS Santanoni Peak
Who to contact: NYS DEC Ray Brook Office

Getting there: From Northway Exit 29 in North Hudson, drive west on the Blue Ridge Road for 17 miles to the right turn for Tahawus. Follow this road, CR 25, to a fork at 6.25 miles. Turn left and continue to a parking area on the right, 9.3 miles north of Blue Ridge Road.

For years the fire tower on Mount Adams languished in disrepair, slowly being dismantled by natural elements. However, the public acquisition of the Tahawus property and the attention this has brought to the mountain has resulted in a surge of renewed interest in the fate of its tower and the stunning panorama of the High Peaks it provides. While most of the mountain will be added to the High Peaks Wilderness, the summit itself will not. This will allow

Opposite: Snowshoeing down the Mount Adams trail

for the retention and repair of the tower, as well as for the retention of this exciting and rewarding hike on the fringe of the High Peaks.

The climb to the summit presents a 1750-foot climb in 2.3 miles of snow-shoeing. Nearly all of that climbing is accomplished in the last 1.6 miles, and the grade only seems to get steeper as you go up, rarely giving you a chance to rest. While by no means a technical climb, it nevertheless earns its difficult rating—Mount Adams is not a place for novices.

Sign in at the register and follow the well-traveled trail for 0.1 mile to the swinging bridge over the Hudson River. At 0.5 mile you cross a boggy bay of Lake Jimmy on a long, low bridge. The woods open up shortly afterwards as you enter a blowdown area, and at 0.7 mile you reach a brown sign pointing uphill to the left. To continue right on the old road would take you to the Opalescent River.

Turning left on the red-marked trail for Mount Adams, you climb for several more minutes out of the blowdown area (caused by Hurricane Floyd in 1999) and cross a graded logging road benched into the side of the mountain. This road is like a boundary between the disturbed woods below and the undisturbed woods that continue the rest of the way to the summit. Cedar, balsam, and birch soon engulf you in their shady cover.

The slope begins moderately, then slowly becomes steep. In a few places you will likely need your hands to help pull yourself up. Views of the mine complex unfold through the trees. In true Adirondack fashion, there are no switchbacks. Why circle around to a gentler approach up the mountain when you can go straight up its steepest side? And so this trail takes the most direct route to the summit.

Only at the summit does the climbing finally ease, a little more than two hours from the start. The tower is located in a small clearing surrounded by dense woods. You only need to climb to the first few landings to see above the trees. There are massive mountains in nearly every direction. The Santanoni Range is to the west, and the Seward and Sawtooth ranges in the distant north-west. Calamity Mountain is the scarred little lump directly below you, and beyond is the trinity of Algonquin, Colden, and Marcy—this three-peaked profile that is so prominent from so many other Adirondack summits here seems to thrust up into the sky. Cliff, Redfield, Skylight, Allen, Cheney Cobble, and Rist mountains round out the expanse of wilderness peaks.

Note that restoration work on the tower was incomplete as of the winter of 2005. Allow an hour and fifteen minutes for the return trek to the trailhead.

Opposite: The Tirrell Pond Lean-to

THE CENTRAL ADIRONDACKS

Many visitors to Adirondack Park are surprised to learn that a significant amount of acreage at the heart of the region is privately owned. Public land is relatively fragmented, but there are several key tracts: the Hoffman Notch Wilderness, the Hudson Gorge Primitive Area, and the Blue Mountain Wild Forest. These are the settings for the following five snowshoe routes.

Compared to the strenuous mountain climbs described in the previous chapter, these routes are much more beginner-friendly. They are also much less crowded. Rolling terrain leads to a number of interior ponds, each one reached by an easy trail marked along the route of an old woods road. The Goodnow Mountain fire tower represents a moderate climb that offers a view of the entire central portion of the Adirondacks, as well as a sweeping panorama of the High Peaks to the north.

A number of small towns dot this area, including Schroon Lake, Indian Lake, Blue Mountain Lake, and Newcomb. The first two in particular are good places to stock up on snacks and supplies before you start your outings. The area is easily accessible from the Northway, I-87. The twin highways of NY 28 and 28N define the southern and northern boundaries of this region, respectively.

--15--
Bailey Pond

Rating: Easy
Round trip: 2.4 miles
Hiking time: 1–2 hours
Starting elevation: 1673 feet
Highest point: 1732 feet
Map: USGS Blue Ridge and Schroon Lake
Who to contact: NYS DEC Warrensburg Office

Getting there: The trailhead is located in Loch Muller, west of Schroon Lake. From Northway (I-87) Exit 28, drive south on US 9 through Schroon Lake Village to Hoffman Road, a right turn. At 6.2 miles you reach Loch Muller Road. Turn right and follow the road for 2.5 miles to the end of the plowing.

Bailey is a small pond at the southern edge of the Hoffman Notch Wilderness Area. It is accessible by a short trail, and although it is only a few miles west of a busy interstate corridor, it really is a wilderness destination. This easy hike with an attractive destination is ideal for families.

Trail to Bailey Pond

The start of this snowshoe route is near a pine tree that was planted by a twelve-year-old boy in 1845. It is easily identified by a plaque. A building near-by was once Warrens Hotel, and there is a good view from the road through Hoffman Notch to the High Peaks.

From the end of Loch Muller Road, follow its unplowed extension past an old fireplace. Bear right at a fork and cross the summer trailhead at 0.2 mile. The register is just inside the woods on the far side. The yellow-marked trail through Hoffman Notch delves straight into the woods, but the trail to Bailey Pond turns left to follow the edge of state land.

Within minutes the foot trail intercepts an old woods road and turns right onto it. There is a long and gentle downhill through a forest of red pine, ending at the West Branch Trout Brook about a mile from the start. The trail hooks left to follow its bank upstream for the final steps to Bailey Pond.

A broad, marshy shoreline surrounds the pond, which is nestled among a series of hills—Hayes Mountain, Cobble Hill, Bailey Hill, and Washburn Ridge, with the steep eastern side of Hayes being the most eye-catching. Together these hills and ridges isolate the pond and make possible its sense of seclusion.

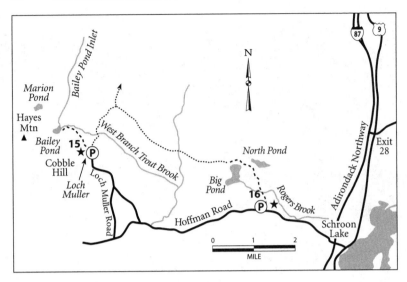

The old road that the trail followed continues further up the valley of Bailey Pond Inlet. You can use it to reach Marion Pond or explore the valley west of Washburn Ridge.

--16--
Big Pond

Rating: Easy
Round trip: 3.2 miles
Hiking time: 2 hours
Starting elevation: 1220 feet
Highest point: 1320 feet
Map: USGS Schroon Lake
Who to contact: NYS DEC Warrensburg Office

Getting there: From Northway (I-87) Exit 28, drive south on US 9 through Schroon Lake Village to Hoffman Road, a right turn. The trailhead is 2.1 miles on the right, with room for two or three cars.

Like Bailey Pond, here is another easy destination in the Hoffman Notch Wilderness. This one is a little longer, but it, too, follows an old woods road. It is a delight for snowshoeing, and it is perfect for those looking for a short, easy excursion through the woods. The route begins in a pine plantation and ends in a native hemlock stand. The pond is a great place for a picnic or a short backpacking trip.

The hike begins next to an old cellar hole buried in the snow. Deer tracks crisscross the snow throughout this pine forest, and the uniform height of its trees suggests that this was once a cleared farm. The trail leads to a wide bridge across Rogers Brook at the foot of a long vly. It then angles northwest through the rolling terrain between Big and North ponds. For the duration of this 1.6-mile hike, you will pass a wide variety of conifers, and so this is an excellent chance to brush up on your dendrology. White pine, Scotch pine, cedar, balsam fir, red spruce, and hemlock all grow beside the trail. Can you identify them?

Just short of an hour the trail enters a tall hemlock stand with Big Pond visible to the left. You have to leave the trail to see the pond, but there is a prominent campsite on the north shore that is ideal for a picnic spot, especially since it faces into the sun and overlooks most of this wild pond.

If you would like to try your hand at a relatively easy bushwhack, consider the route that leads back to the trail by way of the outlet, Rogers Brook. Near the western end of the vly just downstream from the pond, you may find one of the most unusual heron rookeries anywhere. When I last visited it, I

Trail to Big Pond

counted thirty separate nests in only a dozen dead trees—one snag alone bore seven nests. This return bushwhack takes hardly any more time than the hike in along the trail.

--*17*--
Goodnow Mountain

Rating: Moderate
Round trip: 3.4 miles
Hiking time: 2–3 hours
Starting elevation: 1630 feet
Highest point: 2685 feet
Map: USGS Newcomb
Who to contact: NYS DEC Northville Office

Getting there: The trailhead is very easy to find. It is located along NY 28N, 11.4 miles east of Long Lake and 1.5 miles west of the Adirondack Visitor Interpretive Center

Goodnow Mountain is a fire tower mountain located on property owned by SUNY-ESF, the state school of Environmental Sciences and Forestry, just outside of Newcomb. There are no restrictions on public use of the trail, and indeed the school plows the parking area and provides an interpretive booklet to help winter visitors identify some of the natural and historical sites along the trail. The tower is in good shape, and it provides an outstanding view of the High Peaks. The trail climbs about 1050 feet in 1.7 miles.

The interpretive booklets are available at the trailhead register. The trail begins with an initial steep pitch but quickly becomes more gentle. Actually, this is one of the better-developed trails in the Adirondacks, and for the most part the grades remain moderate. Broad switchbacks help in this respect. The trail begins by leading southwest, but it swings more easterly when it intercepts an old road and bears left onto it. From the foundations of an old cabin, there is a very pleasing view of Fishing Brook Mountain.

The trail reaches a saddle between the various summit knobs, where you will find an old horse barn beside the trail. This is a relic of a bygone day, when the mountain's former owner, Archer Huntington, had a camp nearby. The timeworn barn and a well are all that remain now, both merely a curiosity along the trail.

After crossing one of the summit knobs, you pass a small opening to your

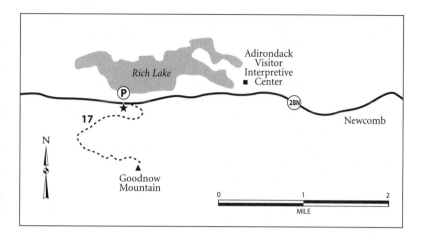

right that affords a view to the south. Puffer, Peaked, and Gore mountains are all visible, many miles away. Much of the intervening territory remains in private ownership, even though this is the heart of the Adirondack Park.

The tower is located just a few minutes beyond. The summit is bald but the surrounding trees grow close enough to obstruct any ground-level views. Therefore, you must climb at least a portion of the tower if you want to see the 360-degree view. The interpretive booklet you picked up at the trailhead contains a sketch of the mountainous horizon in every direction, an invaluable tool in helping you decipher this complex landscape. Be careful climbing the stairs, however, for snow and hoar frost often accumulate on fire towers during the winter.

--28--
Ross, Whortleberry, and Big Bad Luck Ponds

Rating: Moderate
Round trip: 8.1 miles
Hiking time: 4–6 hours
Starting elevation: 1912 feet
Highest point: 1968 feet
Map: USGS Dutton Mountain
Who to contact: NYS DEC Northville Office

Getting there: The trailhead parking area is located 7.8 miles east of Indian Lake on NY 28, where an unnamed spur road forks to the right. This is where you park, but the trailhead itself is about 0.25 mile down NY 28 in the direction of Indian Lake, marked by a brown sign. There is no parking available there.

A branching trail network east of Indian Lake leads to a cluster of secluded ponds, each with its own distinctive character and interesting name. While there may be plenty of ups and downs, this is not a difficult hike. Allow six hours to not only cover the 8.1 miles but also to enjoy each of the three destinations. Trail signs give the distances as 2.5 miles to Ross Pond, and 3 miles each to Whortleberry and Big Bad Luck.

Park at the designated area and walk back along NY 28 to the start of the trail. From the register the red-marked trail plunges into the woods. After cutting through a balsam flat the trail bears right onto an old roadbed that leads in thirty minutes to Bell Mountain Brook, 1 mile from the highway. There is no bridge, but it is a shallow watercourse and not very wide, should you happen to find that it is not frozen.

The longest climb of the hike comes just after this stream crossing. You pass a series of swampy beaver ponds and then at 2.2 miles, after an hour-long

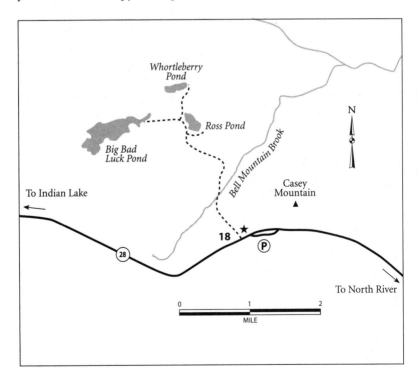

walk, you reach the yellow-marked, 0.3-mile side trail to Ross Pond. This spur leads directly to the side of the pond and then curves around to a scenic campsite on a rocky point. From this one spot it is possible to take in the entire view: hemlock-lined shoreline, small islands, and all.

The main trail continues north, reaching a second intersection just minutes later. To the left is the 0.5-mile, blue-marked spur to Big Bad Luck Pond. It leads through a beautiful pine forest first to a scenic bend on the pond's outlet, and then loops around to the pond itself. Big Bad Luck is the largest of the three, and only a portion is visible from the trail. Its irregular shoreline will almost certainly tempt you to explore it further from the ice, if the conditions are safe.

The main trail ends 0.5 mile north of the Big Bad Luck spur, at a small clearing just out of sight of Whortleberry Pond. There is a plan to extend the trail to a popular campsite near the outlet. From it, you can survey the entire pine-rimmed pond. For now, you can access the pond via a path that leads down to the shore from near the west end of the clearing, or you can bear right through the clearing on a path that approaches the outlet. In winter the first option may be the best, especially if the ice is solid.

Throughout this hike you may see informal signs pointing to unmarked paths. These are segments of the old trail system laid out by a nearby youth camp. When the state marked the main trails, these other routes became redundant. They have no official status, and they will likely become abandoned. Indeed, the signs may be removed to eliminate any confusion.

--19--
Tirrell Pond

Rating: Moderate
Round trip: 9.2 miles
Hiking time: 5–6 hours
Starting elevation: 1850 feet
Highest point: 2000 feet
Map: USGS Deerland and Blue Mountain Lake
Who to contact: NYS DEC Northville Office

Getting there: The trail begins at the well-marked parking area on NY 28 and 30 between Indian Lake and Blue Mountain Lake, near the Lake Durant State Campground. There is ample parking on both sides of the road.

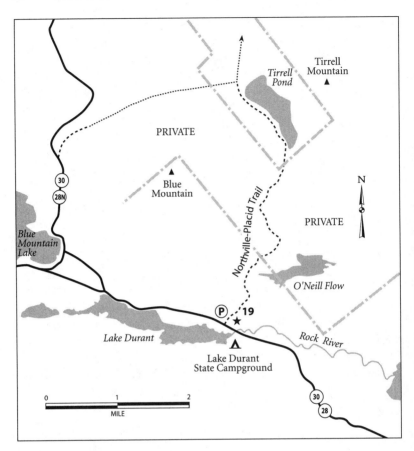

While Tirrell Pond is part of the Forest Preserve, the two most popular accesses to it cross lands that are owned by Finch, Pruyn, and Co., one of the Adirondacks' largest landholders. The timber company has long permitted public access to these two trails, one of which is a section of the 130-mile Northville-Placid Trail. The walk to the pond involves several miles through managed forests, but the woods surrounding the destination are tall and mature. Tirrell Pond is attractively situated at the foot of cliff-scarred Tirrell Mountain.

This 1280-acre parcel comprises the Gospel, School, and Literature lots of Township 19, Totten and Crossfield Purchase, an artifact of the seldom-observed custom among early surveyors of setting aside the heart of each township as public land for income to fund these three public services. Most such lots in other townships remain mere lines on obsolete maps, but in this case the lots eventually became part of the Forest Preserve.

The most interesting approach to the pond is the 4.6-mile section of the Northville-Placid Trail from the south. It takes two and a half hours to hike. Since it is well used, consider this route if your inclination for the day is to follow a hard-packed trail rather than to break through fresh snow somewhere else.

Beginning on state land on the north side of NY 28 and 30, the trail passes through a fine hardwood forest and winds across undulating terrain. Shortly after crossing a finger of O'Neill Flow, you enter the logging company lands, with plenty of signs to remind you not to wander from the trail. A large rock wall looms above the boundary to the left. The trail skirts the flow, but there are no real views. The blue markers then begin to divert you along a series of minor logging roads along the foot of Blue Mountain until once again reaching the Forest Preserve.

There are two lean-tos at Tirrell Pond, one each at the north and south

The outlet of Tirrell Pond

ends. The O'Neill Lean-to stands guard over the outlet of the pond, 3.5 miles and less than two hours from the start. This site is a favorite for the nearby view from the outlet to the rounded cliffs on Tirrell Mountain. The 1.1-mile section of trail north beside the pond is set back from the shoreline, allowing you to sample the fine, mature forest. On the other hand, winter travelers have the option of traveling across the open ice, if conditions permit.

The Tirrell Lean-to, at the pond's north end, is also set back in the woods. The sand beaches nearby make this the campsite of choice for summer visitors, who frequently come in by floatplane as well as by foot. Winter is decidedly the quieter time to visit Tirrell Pond, but this remains a popular hike in all four seasons.

Opposite: Unnamed pond near Raven Lake

THE NORTHWESTERN ADIRONDACKS

The Five Ponds Wilderness, at the heart of the northwestern Adirondack region, has grown with several recent additions and acquisitions to become the third largest wilderness in the park. It is a landscape shaped by glaciers: rich with eskers, kettles, sandy "plains," and more wetlands than can be counted. Mountains are almost nonexistent, and when do you do come across one it seems starkly out of place—Cat Mountain (Hike 20) is a prime example.

The forests of this region are rich and varied, both in terms of their physical nature and their human history. Logging reached this area comparatively late, and at the core of the Five Ponds Wilderness are two separate tracts that were never logged at all. One large tract encompassing many miles of the Oswegatchie River was logged by the Rich Lumber Company during the World War I era. Rather than floating their logs to mill, the company constructed a series of railroads that led into the heart of the forest, including the one to Dead Creek Flow, which forms part of Hike 20.

The company maintained a somewhat tenuous coexistence with the guides who led "sports" up the river to fish. The guides' primary request was that the company not harvest the tall white pines that shaded the prized trout pools on the river. However, when one lumberman had a dispute with the company, his method of revenge was to cut the pines at High Falls.

The company established Wanakena as its base of operations, and this little company town faced a major crisis when the lumbermen closed shop and moved to New England. Most of the lands became part of the Forest Preserve, and the state established what is now the SUNY-ESF Ranger School, which is by far Wanakena's largest employer. Thus, the village survives today.

Even after the lumber company left, this forest did not fare well in the twentieth century. Soon after being logged, much of the area was severely burned. Then there was the Big Blow of 1950, which leveled forests throughout the Adirondacks. However, it was the massive windstorm of 1995 that essentially redefined the character of the wilderness. Make no mistake, this is a vast, wild, and rugged territory, one that still retains a strange beauty despite the blowdown.

The western Adirondacks catch nearly all of the lake-effect snowstorms that come off of Lake Ontario, and so snowfall accumulations have the potential to be quite deep. Snowmobiling is popular, with major corridor trails that encircle the wilderness interior. Some of these "trails" are actually the roads you will be driving. The most notable of these is the road to Stillwater (Hike 22) where cars may well be outnumbered by snowmobiles on the weekends.

There are several approaches to the fringes of this area, with many routes that lend themselves to snowshoeing. Most of these, however, involve bushwhacking. The routes that I have selected will take you away from the motorized corridors and into the quieter recesses of the winter forest.

I have also added a fourth trail that, while not part of the Adirondacks, is reasonably close by and should not be overlooked by snowshoers. Whetstone Gulf State Park is part of the Tug Hill region, which lies between Lake Ontario and the Adirondacks. Because of this, it is even snowier than the Adirondacks. Tug Hill is legendary among snowmobilers and cross-country skiers, but it is short on the types of destinations that would attract snowshoers. Whetstone Gulf is an exception, and one that will please beginning and experienced snowshoers alike.

--20--
Cat Mountain Pond

Rating: Moderate
Round trip: 11.2 miles
Hiking time: 6 hours or 2 days
Starting elevation: 1496 feet
Highest point: 1900 feet
Map: USGS Newton Falls, Five Ponds, and Wolf Mountain
Who to contact: NYS DEC Potsdam Office

Getting there: The trailhead is located in Wanakena, which is reached by taking CR 61 south from NY 3 between Cranberry Lake and Star Lake. Bear right at the first two forks and cross the Oswegatchie River. The parking area is 0.5 mile after the bridge, to the right of the road.

Cat Mountain Pond lies at the foot of the 500-foot cliffs of its namesake mountain; it is readily accessible by trail; and it is surrounded by a cluster of other small ponds. Despite all this, it is not generally seen as a destination in itself, but merely as something to look at from the summit of Cat Mountain.

Actually, Cat Mountain Pond is one of the most attractive bodies of water anywhere in the Adirondacks, and it makes an ideal base camp for a winter overnight. Most people who snowshoe in this area head just to Cat Mountain, and few take the time to go on to Cowhorn and Bassout ponds. Together with Glasby Pond, which you inevitably pass while hiking to any of the other places, there is enough to see in this one location—four ponds and the mountain—to make it worthy of planning an entire weekend, taking your time as you explore all the ins and outs.

The trail begins by following the beds of one of the Rich Lumber Company's railroads, passing through haunting spruce swamps that alternate with patches of blowdown. A brisk forty-five-minute walk suffices for the trek to Dead Creek Flow. The trail loops around the end of the flow—a bay of Cranberry Lake—but in winter it is possible to cut a corner here by crossing directly to the Janacks Landing Lean-to. This shaves about 0.6 mile off of the distances noted below. The lean-to is named for a former fire tower observer from Cat Mountain who lived near here with his family.

From the flow the trail climbs gradually to an intersection at 3.9 miles, where you should bear left onto the yellow-marked trail. It climbs for another 0.3 mile to Glasby Pond, circles its south shore, and then climbs to the

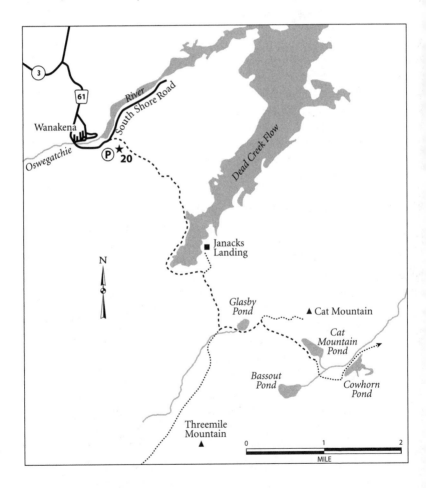

Cat Mountain cliffs over Cat Mountain Pond

intersection with the Cat Mountain trail at 4.6 miles. The trail sees much less winter use beyond this point, as it crosses a shoulder of the mountain. It takes a zigzagging course through the blowdown towards the pond, which you first see at 5.6 miles. There is a designated campsite near the outlet at the east end, but the attractive woods near the west end are open enough to permit you to establish your own low-impact tent site. You will have the whole pond for your front yard, and the nesting ravens on Cat Mountain for neighbors. You may well even spot a bobcat prowling about the area.

Bassout Pond is a short side trip away, reached by an easy bushwhack; there is a good spring near its northernmost corner. Cowhorn Pond sits in seclusion on the far side of a tall esker and boasts its own lean-to. And, of course, there is the trail to the summit of Cat Mountain itself. In terms of exploring the whole area, though, Cat Mountain Pond is the most attractive and centrally located destination, from which you could easily explore all of these other places as side trips.

--21--
West Branch Oswegatchie Headwaters

Rating: Most Difficult
Round trip: 11 miles
Hiking time: 8 hours minimum
Starting elevation: 1431 feet
Highest point: 1720 feet
Map: USGS Stillwater, Oswegatchie SW & SE
Who to contact: NYS DEC Lowville Office

Getting there: The start of this hike is at the end of winter maintenance on Long Pond Road. From NY 812 in Croghan, turn east onto Belfort Road and follow it to the hydro project on the Beaver River. Across the bridge, turn right onto Long Pond Road and follow it for 10.3 miles to its end, near the Berggrens Hunting Club.

What this snowshoe route offers is a chance to explore a corner of the Adirondacks that seems half forest and half wetland. There are two little-used trails that penetrate the area, and the 11-mile loop that connects the two ends of those trails—with a bushwhack in the middle—is an exceptional route that can only be done as a winter snowshoe hike.

Rather than taking you to one specific destination, this loop connects an

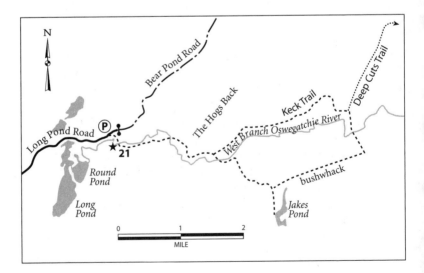

entire series of little beaver flows, bogs filled with black spruce, small ponds, and secluded streams. As such, it is best done while the wilderness is in the throes of a frigid winter. By the time the spring thaw arrives, it will be impassable. Even as a summer hiking route, without the bushwhack portion, these trails can be muddy and wet.

The terrain is remote and rugged, and the miles are long. Get an early start and be sure to bring company—this is not a place where you would want to be stuck alone.

A red-marked foot trail begins at the south side of the parking area at the end of Long Pond Road; its first 1.6 miles are an easement through private land. This section crosses the West Branch of the Oswegatchie twice on high footbridges, the second time at the foot of a sprawling wetland. The trail is parallel to the river but generally set back from it, shaded by a variety of conifer stands, including at least one swampy grove of tall black spruce. The trail reaches state land at 1.6 miles.

The trail splits at 2 miles, where for now you should bear left on the yellow-marked Keck Trail. This route continues to parallel the West Branch, although you have to leave the trail to see the river. The trail leads through the valley for 3.1 miles, passing a number of beaver flows—active and otherwise—along the way. At the end of those 3.1 miles, it hooks more northerly to become the Deep Cuts Trail. A few aging signs mark this intersection.

Leave the marked trail here, following an unmarked route at the southeast corner of the intersection. This was once the access to the Deep Cuts Camp, now just a clearing in the woods. The path narrows and reaches the river 0.3 mile from the marked trail, or 5.4 miles overall. This basin of spruce, pine, and fir is a gem.

There has in the past been a small bridge here over the West Branch Oswegatchie, although it is not an official structure. A path continues for another 0.4 mile into the woods southeast of the river, ending abruptly at an obscure swamp. Explore this series of little wetlands and open beaver ponds, and then set off on a bushwhack course of due west. The forest is rugged, dense, and beautiful. Eventually you will reach a large wetland complex with some of the best black spruce stands in the western Adirondacks. Use them as your guide back towards the Jakes Pond trail.

Jakes Pond itself is a small S-shaped sliver of water with steep banks. By trail, it is a 4.1-mile, two-hour walk back to the trailhead. The trail crosses a large wetland at 0.9 mile, and then a series of smaller wetlands on its route to yet another footbridge over the Oswegatchie. Just beyond is the intersection with the Keck Trail, and the final 2 miles of your long hike ends as it began.

--22--
Wilderness Lakes Tract

Rating: Difficult
Round trip: 10 miles
Hiking time: 5–7 hours
Starting elevation: 1722 feet
Highest point: 2078 feet
Map: USGS Stillwater
Who to contact: NYS DEC Lowville Office

Getting there: Stillwater is very far removed from the nearest state highway. From NY 12 in Lowville, turn east onto River Street. In 4.4 miles you reach Bushes Landing, where you should bear left onto Number Four Road. Follow it for 13.6 miles, where signs will point right toward Stillwater. Pavement ends shortly after this turn, and the remaining 9 miles to Stillwater can be quite dicey for driving if there is a snowstorm in progress. There is a spacious parking area at Stillwater, as well as a forest ranger. The trailhead, however, is 1.3 miles north at the end of Necessary Dam Road. The trailhead is not plowed, and it is difficult to park without blocking access to the Stillwater dam, so it may be better to park in Stillwater and walk to this point.

This is a route that would seem to be ideal for cross-country skiing, but in my observations it seems to be the snowshoers who visit this area the most. In 1990 the state acquired full title to a forestry parcel named the Wilderness Lakes Tract, an important acquisition because of the many ponds it contains. It also consolidated the state's Forest Preserve holdings north of the Stillwater Reservoir. The land was heavily logged in the final years preceding state ownership, and the Wilderness Lakes Tract is crisscrossed by a series of wide logging roads that will be with us for years to come.

However, despite certain aesthetic shortcomings, the area is a magnet for pond-hoppers—people who enjoy bouncing around the backcountry by traveling from one pond to the next. In the warmer half of the year, small pack canoes are the vehicle of choice, but in the winter you can get by with a much smaller load. A pair of snowshoes will suffice. While the bushwhacking possibilities are too numerous to list—just look at the map—there is a series of marked canoe carries that will take you into the heart of the area. Wait until the ponds have had a chance to freeze adequately, and go!

From the end of Necessary Dam Road and the unplowed trailhead, cross

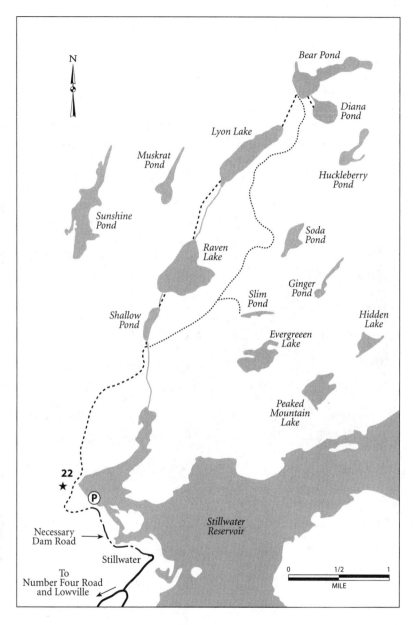

the wide bridge over the Beaver River, just below the dam. The first leg of the route follows the Raven Lake Primitive Corridor, an active right-of-way that leads to a tiny inholding on the south shore of Raven Lake. Walking this road may seem rather dull, but it is safer than the alternative, which entails crossing the reservoir and picking up the canoe carry trail at Kettle Hole Bay. The road is 2 miles long and includes three long uphill grades.

When the road approaches the outlet of Shallow Pond, the best part of the trip begins. Look for the brown sign pointing left for the canoe carry, which leads to a point where you should be able to step safely onto the pond—just be sure to avoid the soft ice that typically surrounds the outlet itself. Shallow Pond leads north to Raven Lake, and where the pond narrows into a channel the width of a stream, cut inland through the woods to avoid another patch of soft ice.

Raven Lake is surrounded by rolling hills, with the one private cabin on

Snapping a picture near Raven Lake

its south shore. Walk into the northern bay of the lake, where the inlet flows in. Look for a small sign to the left, marking the next 0.8-mile trail segment to Lyon Lake. It follows an old logging road up a gentle grade to the outlet of that next lake, which is 0.7 mile long with a few tall white pines on its west side.

Cross the length of Lyon Lake and find the next carry trail, which connects with Bear Pond. This is a whistle-shaped body of water with several rustic camps on its privately owned north shore. However, a short distance east of the Lyon Pond carry, you will find one last trail segment leading across a narrow spit of land to Diana Pond, the last of the chain.

Inevitably, some snowshoers will want to try and reach some of the other ponds that are tucked away in the nearby woods. Generally speaking, the area south and east of this chain is where the heaviest logging occurred, and where you are likely to encounter pockets of dense brush. You will also come across the logging roads there, which all ultimately lead back to Raven Lake. West of the canoe carries, the woods are more open. Muskrat and Sunshine ponds are very attractive destinations, each one sitting in a pine-filled basin.

--23--
Whetstone Gulf

Rating:	Easy/Moderate
Round trip:	5 miles
Hiking time:	3 hours
Starting elevation:	1330 feet
Highest point:	1900 feet
Map:	USGS Glenfield, Page
Who to contact:	Whetstone Gulf State Park

Getting there: Whetstone Gulf State Park is located 5.6 miles south of Lowville on NY 26. Follow the signs onto West Road, and the park entrance is then the very first left turn. Parking is at the far end of the complex, next to the Beach House.

Whetstone Gulf is one of New York's oldest state parks. Located on the eastern edge of the Tug Hill Plateau, the gulf is a deep and winding gully eroded into the layered bedrock, 3 miles long and at times several hundred feet deep. The park benefits from the region's typically copious snowfall amounts, and it is maintained from December 15 to March 15 for winter hikers. There is no fee. Skiers love Whetstone Gulf for the miles of groomed trails winding through

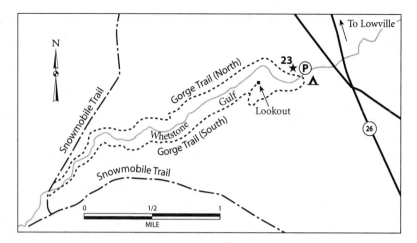

the campground, but only a few venture toward the gorge itself. That is terrain best suited for snowshoeing.

As a route for cross-country skiing, the trail around the rim of the gorge bears an expert rating. Indeed, there are frequent signs all along that trail warning hikers of the potential dangers of the gorge, the walls of which are very steep. The rim trail hugs the forested edge of the gorge and may make certain hikers feel very uneasy. Nevertheless, it is a scenic hike, even more so in winter when the trees are bare and the views thus easier to come by.

Despite its proximity to the precipice, which is entirely screened by trees, the trail itself is suitable for novice snowshoers who have a healthy amount of common sense. There is a long climb from the campground to the rim, but beyond that the trail remains virtually level. And although the entire loop around the gorge is about 5 miles long, hikers have the option in this case of going only as far as they wish and turning around when they are ready. Additionally, there is a high chance that you will see deer near the beginning, and the Beach House at the trailhead serves as a warming hut every Wednesday through Sunday until the first week in March.

The south side of the Gorge Trail begins near the Beach House, and it is well marked with warning signs. Among the warnings is one stating that no one should be setting off after 3:00 PM. The trail at once begins its long climb towards the rim, following a wide road grade through a plantation of red pine. As tiring as the climb may be, think how fun it will be to sail back down on the return! The trail loops inland around a tributary, and after twenty minutes reaches an intersection at the rim.

Opposite: Whetstone Gulf

A right turn will bring you to a lookout, a viewing platform overlooking the Black River valley. Note that this side trail, only 0.1 mile long, traverses a narrow hogsback ridge with drop-offs on both sides. The Gorge Trail is a left turn, and it closely follows the rim. Remember to keep back from the edge, for the drop is sudden and steep. At nearly every major bend there is an open vista. A number of these places invite a picnic in the snow.

As you proceed upstream, the north rim inches ever closer to the south rim, until you reach a vista of the gorge's steepest, most dramatic section. The walls are too steep here for vegetation, and the rock strata stick out through the patches of snow. The stream makes a sharply zigzagging course through the V-cut gulf. The woods become much more dense, and when next you have a clear view of the stream as you proceed west the gulf has become merely a wooded ravine. The trail ends at 2.5 miles at the unplowed Carrigan Hill Road, and hikers who have ventured this far have the option of either turning back here or turning right across the bridge to return via the Northern Trail to make the 5-mile loop.

Opposite: Snags near Cotton Lake

SOUTHWESTERN ADIRONDACK LAKES
AND PONDS

The southwestern Adirondacks represent the corner of the park with which I am most familiar. This is the area closest to where I live, and it was the area in which I first developed a taste for canoeing, hiking, and snowshoeing. Within these woods are dozens of ponds and other enticing destinations, and in many cases the access points are scarcely an hour's drive from the city of Utica. Yet, for the most part, this area is overlooked by many hikers and snowshoers. I attribute that to a number of factors, such as a shortage of foot trails and the fact that the trailheads are often secreted in out-of-the-way places.

The appeal of the southwestern Adirondacks is almost entirely in its ponds—there are few ridges of note. This was an area logged at an early date. The woodsmen built a network of primitive roads through the forest, made their mark, and then left. Much of the area returned to state ownership, creating large, contiguous tracts of wilderness-quality lands. The forest has been regenerating ever since then, leaving very few signs of the former disturbances.

Beyond the state land, many of the older routes in this area lead toward the private holdings of the Adirondack League Club. Formed in 1890, this club attracted wealthy individuals who wanted to establish a private park deep within the heart of the North Woods. At its height the club owned well over a hundred thousand acres of forests and lakes, but over the years a sizable portion of this has found its way into the public domain. The Adirondack League Club still posts many thousands of acres of land, but its holdings now consist of two isolated tracts.

There are strong similarities between the six snowshoe routes described in this chapter. They are all close to the same length; they all encounter rolling terrain, but few hills of any note; and they all end at a pond. However, no two Adirondack ponds are ever alike, and that is just as true here. Middle Settlement Lake, south of Old Forge, offers a scenic lean-to for camping and picnicking. Stone Dam and Little Woodhull are delightful little places rimmed with lush spruce-fir stands, where the chance for solitude is a pretty good probability. While Cotton, DeBraine, and Trout lakes are not any more remote than the others, they present navigational challenges since they have no marked trails.

I have picked all of these destinations because they are places to which I have returned time and again. They have an excellent quality of conveying the snowshoer into seemingly deep wilderness over modest distances.

--*24*--
Middle Settlement Lake

Rating: Moderate
Round trip: 6.4 miles
Hiking time: 3–4 hours
Starting elevation: 1742 feet
Highest point: 1870 feet
Map: USGS Thendara
Who to contact: NYS DEC Herkimer Office

Getting there: The trailhead is located on NY 28, 3 miles south of the Thendara train station. There is a large parking area on the east side of the road. The trail starts on the west side of the road, marked by a brown sign.

Middle Settlement Lake is the star attraction of the 26,528-acre Ha-de-ron-dah Wilderness, an area that was severely burned by forest fires many decades ago. The landscape was denuded by that fire, making it worthless to its owners, who ultimately sold it to the state. The forest has since grown back to reclaim

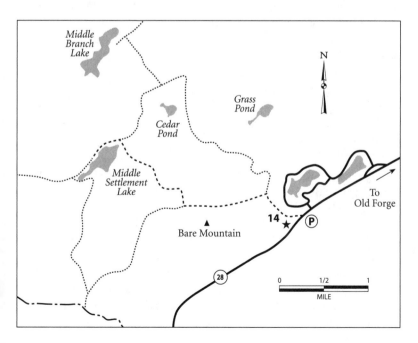

Peering into the rock shelter near Middle Settlement Lake

the valleys, hills and shorelines, although in terms of the slow life processes of trees the forest is still in an early stage of succession.

The name Ha-de-ron-dah is supposedly a more accurate spelling of the original Indian word meaning "bark eater"—the phrase that eventually morphed into "Adirondack," although no one is sure of the true origin of the word. According to the story, the Mohawks once observed their Algonquin enemies eating bark one harsh season in the Adirondack region when they ran out of sources of food, and derided them as "bark eaters."

When Emmons first proposed the name "Adirondack" as the name for the High Peaks after his 1837 expedition to Mount Marcy, most people referred to this portion of the region only as John Browns Tract. In fact, the original road to Old Forge passed through what is now the Ha-de-ron-dah Wilderness. The Browns Tract Road was little more than a rough wagon track, even in its heyday. Accounts from that period suggest that it was more comfortable to walk the road than to ride in any wheeled vehicle. It now forms a portion of the hike to Middle Settlement Lake.

From the highway, the route to Middle Settlement Lake begins on a red-marked trail and almost immediately begins a steep, tiresome climb. This hill is infamous among all hikers heading to Middle Settlement, and it may leave you dreading what might follow. There is no need to worry, for there are no further hills even remotely as steep as this. The trail is forced to take this route to avoid private land.

At 0.6 mile, bear left onto a yellow-marked trail—the Browns Tract Road, such as it is. Follow it for 0.9 mile, where you need to turn right onto a blue-marked trail. This leads past an open beaver meadow on the right and then makes an easy climb over a hillside forested with tall black cherry trees and other hardwoods. The preponderance of black cherry trees is one of the telltale signs of the forest fire, for these trees would not grow well in the shade of other trees.

This blue trail leads to a second yellow trail, where you bear left for the lake and the lean-to. (All of these intersections have directional signs.) A massive rock face rises above this intersection, and several cabin-sized boulders lie at its base. There is a natural rock shelter located within this talus pile—a crawl space under one of the rocks where people have camped in the past. Bear left on the yellow trail, reaching the northeast end of Middle Settlement Lake just moments later.

The trail skirts around the north side of the lake to the lean-to that sits atop a rock bluff, about midway down the shore. Many winter visitors forego the trail at this point and cross the ice directly to the shelter. This lean-to is perfectly situated to allow its occupants to really enjoy this pretty place, and it is a rare weekend at any time of the year when no one comes by to pay it a visit. Middle Settlement is typical of this region's lakes in that the open hardwood forest marches right down to the water's edge, especially on the south shore. The red spruce and balsam fir that most people associate with ponds in the North Country are here represented in small numbers. You will find evidence that beaver have been out and about almost everywhere you look.

--25--
Stone Dam Lake

Rating: Moderate
Round trip: 7 miles
Hiking time: 3–4 hours
Starting elevation: 1460 feet
Highest point: 1700 feet
Map: USGS North Wilmurt
Who to contact: NYS DEC Herkimer Office

Getting there: From NY 28 in Forestport, turn east onto Woodhull Street toward the Buffalo Head Restaurant. At the fork just before the restaurant and railroad tracks, bear left. This is North Lake Road. It enters Adirondack Park at the Herkimer County line and reaches the Stone Dam Trailhead 6.5 miles past the railroad. If it is not snowing, you can park on the shoulder. Otherwise the nearest plowed parking area is at Mulchy Spring, another half mile up the road.

Stone Dam is an all-around good hike: a fine trail, beautiful woods, and a pretty destination. It is a beguiling little place where, if the conditions are right, you could pass a few hours poking around in the wetlands that surround the pond.

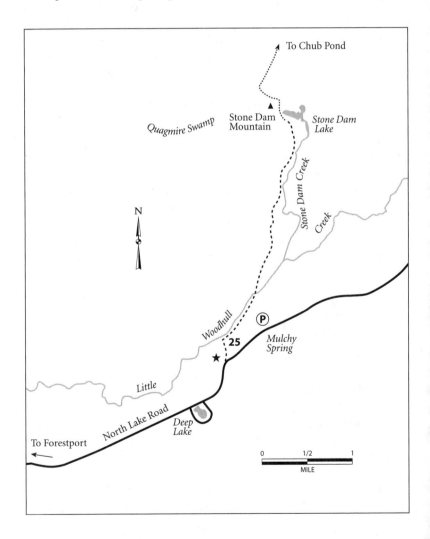

Indeed, winter may be *the* time to visit Stone Dam. The spruce and balsam that line its shores make this the exception for ponds in this area, although it is a welcome exception. It is a wild, lonely place that is hardly 3 miles, as the crow flies, from the Adirondack Park boundary.

The trail to Stone Dam Lake is straightforward and completely uncomplicated, for there are no intersections or special turns to watch for. It leads north from North Lake Road, reaching a narrow footbridge over Little Woodhull Creek in 0.6 mile, or twenty minutes from the start. This is a stream that rarely freezes over completely, and it is usually interesting to observe the ice patterns below the bridge.

Beyond, the trail parts company with the stream, favoring a course that keeps more to the west. In fact, the USGS map is inaccurate in its portrayal of the trail. The map shows

Wooded shoreline of Stone Dam Lake

it more or less following the side of Stone Dam Creek, when actually the route keeps well away from that stream or any other, keeping instead high on the side of the hills. The map labels one hill as Stone Dam Mountain, suggesting that the surveyor had a sense of humor. None of the local hills even vaguely resemble mountains.

After making a point of avoiding the lowlands and climbing the hillside, the trail begins to drop in stages as it slowly approaches the pond. Again the map is incorrect, for the trail only glances past the west of the pond, rather than curving sinuously around its shoreline. The trail draws no closer than a hundred feet of the pond, continuing north to eventually reach Chub Pond. Leave the trail at this point to visit Stone Dam.

The north shore of the pond is a peninsula of sorts, with a large wetland to the north. This point of land is densely wooded, and it can be rather tough trying to follow it to look for the site of the former Stone Dam Lake Camp. This camp was really just a tiny lean-to, now overgrown with trees and probably impossible to find in winter. It hailed from the day when it was possible for anyone to get a permit from the Conservation Department to build a shelter on state land.

The south shore of the pond is much more open and hiker-friendly, and of course it leads to the long outlet channel, where you will find the remains of the stone dam.

--26--
Little Woodhull Lake

Rating: Moderate
Round trip: 6.6 miles
Hiking time: 3–4 hours
Starting elevation: 1772 feet
Highest point: 1988 feet
Map: USGS Honnedaga Lake
Who to contact: NYS DEC Herkimer Office

Getting there: The trailhead is on North Lake Road. From the village of Forestport, turn east from NY 28 at the north end of the bridge over the Black River. Drive for 1.2 miles to the Buffalo Head Restaurant, where the road forks. The left fork is North Lake Road, and the trailhead is 13.1 miles further, on the left side of the road. The only signs marking the trail are set back in the woods, but the trail itself is obvious. There is year-round parking 100 feet further on the right.

Little Woodhull Lake is another of the secluded ponds hidden in the rolling terrain near North Lake Road. This one is accessed via an old snowmobile trail that for many years has seen more foot travel in winter than snowmobiles. In fact, it is one of my favorite hikes, as it leads through quiet forests to a handsome destination, and I rarely encounter anyone else. In addition, there are other sites around the lake to investigate, such as neighboring Lily Lake and the broad meadows surrounding the outlet. These are places that are easier to reach and enjoy in winter.

I enjoy exploring the lake from its frozen surface as much as I do from a canoe in the summer, and it is interesting to compare the two seasons at the lake. In the warmer months, Little Woodhull appears as a shallow, boggy place, its surface nearly filled in with bog mats that float just below the surface of the water. When the water turns cold in the fall, these mats sink into the depths, and the lake again appears to be an open sheet of water. On one early

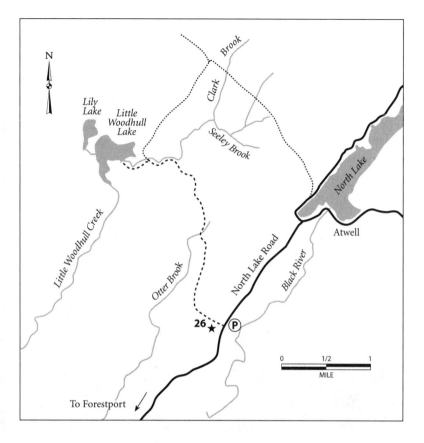

winter visit, I found the whole surface to be a sheet of solid, glare ice with no snow to cover it—a perfect skating rink from shore to shore.

The 3.3-mile trail presents the snowshoer with few obstacles. For the first 2 miles the route travels along a long-abandoned woods road, with only a few short grades to add some diversity to the terrain. Look for a sharp right turn after thirty minutes or more of walking, partly obscured by old blowdown. After 2 miles the trail passes the side of a wide wetland, off to the right. This is Little Woodhull Creek, the primary tributary of the lake. It is fed by a series of small streams that somehow give it a remarkably consistent flow, rising and dropping very little from winter to summer.

Just 0.4 mile later, you reach an intersection with the red-marked trail to North Lake. Continue straight on the yellow trail, which delves into the balsam woods for the final 0.3-mile approach to the lake. This section is as fine a walk as any described in this guide—breathe deeply the aromatic air. The trail

Late afternoon sky over the outlet of Little Woodhull Lake

ends at the south end of the lake, at a small clearing that serves just fine as a lunch spot.

As mentioned above, winter hikers have the advantage of being able to set out across the ice to explore the expansive meadows along the outlet, and to make the short trek over to Lily Lake. It takes three hours at the least to make the round-trip hike, but by exploring the lake's environs this outing can be extended to fill most of a day.

--27--
Twin Lakes

Rating: Moderate
Round trip: 6.4 miles
Hiking time: 3 hours
Starting elevation: 1673 feet
Highest point: 1968 feet
Map: USGS North Wilmurt, Morehouseville
Who to contact: NYS DEC Herkimer Office

Getting there: From NY 28 in Forestport, turn east onto Woodhull Street toward the Buffalo Head Restaurant. At the fork just before the restaurant and railroad tracks, bear left. This is North Lake Road. It enters Adirondack Park at the Herkimer County line and reaches Farr Road (a right turn) 10 miles from the railroad tracks. Farr Road immediately crosses the Black River, and the trailhead is on the left at 0.6 mile, just

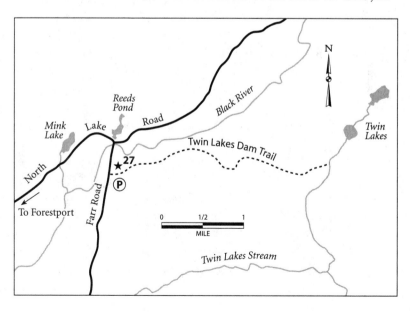

before a small camp. There is no sign, but road crews usually clear a small turnout for parking.

New York State—and City, for that matter—rose to economic prominence in the nineteenth century largely on the success of the Erie Canal. It was the Erie that connected the city with the Great Lakes, making it a port not just for the Northeast, but for the land-locked Midwest as well. This created a pragmatic urgency to create an Adirondack Park and Forest Preserve, since the mountains were viewed as a source of water for the canal, and clear-cutting was considered a threat to the forest's ability to hold and slowly release water runoff.

In the southwestern Adirondacks, the state built a series of reservoirs intended to feed the Black River and Erie canals. Of the so-called Canal Lakes, all but two are still in existence. The smallest dam, at Twin Lakes, was breached decades ago; only part of its stone sluiceway remains.

The trail to Twin Lakes is a lightly used, rolling route leading from Farr Road straight to the dam. The lakes are now two small pools surrounded by acres of open wetlands. In summer it can be difficult to walk through these

Remains of the stone dam at Twin Lakes

boggy areas, but snowshoers will have no problem at all exploring the farthest reaches of the old reservoir. Despite the human history, Twin Lakes offer an outstanding wilderness setting and a sense of seclusion.

From Farr Road, the trail leads east, following an old woods road marked with yellow disks. There are many short ups and downs, but no steep hills for miles around. While the walk through these quiet woods is very pleasant, the first 2 miles are uneventful. This changes when the trail dips into a small valley filled with balsam and crosses an open vly. (If necessary, cross on the beaver dam in the woods to the right.) After rising through a glen and cutting across a low ridge, the trail ends near the foot of the old reservoir. The dam is a short distance to the right, and the lakes are further out in the open wetlands.

If you have snowshoed here during a thaw, you should also check out the series of waterfalls that mark the first 0.4 mile of the outlet stream below the dam. There are a number of cascades, with Hole-in-the-Wall Falls and November Falls being the largest. They do not appear on any topo maps, and you must bushwhack to find them.

There are stories that lumbermen would come to Twin Lakes when the state officials weren't around and release water from the dam to bolster their spring log drives down the Black River. Perhaps the most interesting outdoorsman associated with this region is Addie Reed, who lived with his mother and brother at a homestead at Reeds Pond. Crippled by polio as a child, Addie was nevertheless an avid outdoorsman. He would pull himself through the woods by his hands and was known to travel miles at a time this way. He and his brother lived at Reeds Pond most of their lives; their home site is now a summer camping area.

--28--
Cotton Lake

Rating: Difficult
Round trip: 7 miles
Hiking time: 4 hours
Starting elevation: 1710 feet
Highest point: 1910 feet
Map: USGS North Wilmurt, Morehouseville
Who to contact: NYS DEC Herkimer Office

Getting there: From NY 28 in Forestport, turn east onto Woodhull Street toward the Buffalo Head Restaurant. At the fork just before the restaurant and railroad tracks, bear left. This is North Lake Road. It enters Adirondack Park at the Herkimer County line and reaches Farr Road (a right turn) 10 miles from the railroad tracks. Farr Road leads to North Wilmurt in 2.2 miles, where you bear left onto Withers Road. At 0.6 mile, where the road swings left, the old woods road to Cotton Lake begins on the right. You have to park on the shoulder, but as this is a lightly used dead-end road, there is little traffic to disrupt.

What makes the snowshoe route to Cotton Lake difficult is not its 3.5-mile length or the rolling terrain, but simply the fact that the place is reached only by navigating a series of unmarked old woods roads. Further complicating matters is the fact that none of these roads show on topographic maps. However, this

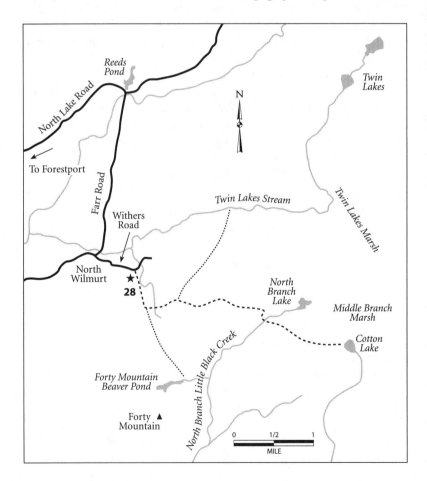

Cotton Lake shoreline

has long been a favorite winter hike of mine, for not only is it close to where I live but the entire route is located in deep woods with a true wilderness quality. Even the trailhead is remote and secluded. This hike is sure to please.

The old woods road begins clearly enough at the bend on Withers Road. For the first fifteen minutes of walking it leads nearly due south, but then makes a prominent bend to the east. Just after the bend, there is a lesser side road continuing south towards Forty Mountain Beaver Pond. Continue straight as the trail swings just north of east, reaching another fork at 1 mile. You may notice an old barrel or gas can just before this point. You may also notice two or three diverging routes. The leftmost leads to private land; straight leads to the site of a stone dam on Twin Lakes Stream; right is the route to Cotton Lake.

For the remaining 2.5 miles to the pond, the route winds between a series of open and partially wooded wetlands, several of which you can see from the path. You then swing southeast and begin a long descent into the valley of the North Branch Little Black Creek. (On the return, this is the longest uphill on the entire route.) Find a good ice bridge across the North Branch and follow the route around the north side of another vly visible to your right.

The path then forks left from the old road. This turn may be marked by an old paint blaze or other informal marking, but for the remaining 0.3 mile the path no longer follows a woods road and is therefore less obvious. It leads up one rise, skirts the edge of a slight basin, and then climbs to a saddle. Cotton Lake is just beyond, after a nearly two-hour hike.

The pond is small and round, and might be considered plain were it not for the sculpture garden of weathered snags that rim its southern and eastern shoreline. The gently sloping topography and the open forest make it possible to establish a winter camp just about anywhere around the pond. The sense of seclusion is hard to beat. Bushwhackers will also be tempted to continue on to Middle Branch Marsh and North Branch Lake, both of which are much easier to explore in the frozen embrace of winter.

--29--
DeBraine and Trout Lakes

Rating: Difficult
Round trip: 5.2 miles
Hiking time: 3 hours
Starting elevation: 1896 feet
Highest point: 2244 feet
Map: USGS Morehouse Lake
Who to contact: NYS DEC Herkimer Office

Getting there: From NY 8 in Hoffmeister, across from the post office, turn south onto French Road. Follow it south for 1.3 miles to Farm Road, a left turn. Only the first 200 feet or so of this road are plowed, giving access to a private driveway. Provided you don't block the driveway, there is plenty of parking.

Like Cotton Lake (Hike 28), the real difficulty in getting to DeBraine and Trout lakes lies mostly in the fact that the route to them is not a marked trail. Actually, if the state were to adopt this route as one of its own, DeBraine would be a very easy but rewarding destination. Trout would earn a moderate rating. As it currently stands, DeBraine is still an easy trip for anyone comfortable hiking without the benefit of directional signs and markers. The continuing path to Trout Lake earns its difficult rating, especially in winter, when the route can be harder to detect.

DeBraine is a relatively recent Forest Preserve acquisition, and you will

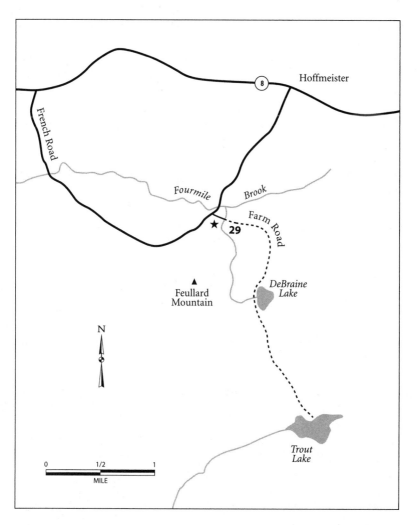

find the remains of a camp protruding from the snow near its western shore. In addition to opening the beautiful pond to the public, this purchase also provided better access to a tract of old growth forest to the south, encompassing Trout Lake. This tract extends south and east to the Powley-Piseco Road and used to contain several celebrated stands of red spruce. Of all the Adirondack trees besides white pine, red spruce was the most sought-after for lumber in the nineteenth century. It is a slow-growing species, and while many formerly logged areas have had a chance to return to near old growth proportions, it is only in the true old growth stands—those that were never logged—where you might be lucky to find individual trees that surpass the average size for the species.

The tragedy is that red spruce is particularly susceptible to environmental changes, and most of the full-sized trees here in the Ferris Lake Wild Forest and adjoining areas are rapidly dying off. Whether the cause is acid rain or some biological factor, the end result is a forest that has lost its most distinguishing constituents. When I first hiked to Trout Lake in 2000, I measured one mammoth spruce tree with a diameter of nearly 33 inches at breast height. It died sometime late in 2001.

This snowshoe route begins by following the unplowed portion of Farm Road to its end, a distance of only 0.5 mile. It is easy to see where this road got its name; the former pastures are only in the early stages of reverting to forest. It might be interesting to check the animal tracks in this open area and compare them to what you will find later in the deep woods. The road ends in a turnaround loop.

The path to the lakes begins from the southeast corner of the turnaround loop, leading south to cross a small stream. Beyond, it climbs a small hill through a young, cut-over stand of hardwoods. If there has been a heavy snow recently, these may be bowed across the trail, making it a little harder to find your way. Just 0.2 mile from the end of Farm Road, you reach a fork. The way right leads up, whereas the route to the lakes bears left, descending to the edge of the long vly north of DeBraine Lake.

The approach to DeBraine is one of the most pleasing of any trail in the Adirondacks, in any season, all after just a 1.1-mile, twenty-minute snowshoe trek. The trail approaches the lake's north shore and skirts its edge to the site of the cabin, and nothing is hidden from the view. It is a delightful place, and you will be amazed by how a pretty pond so easy to get to can seem so remote and wild.

The trip to Trout Lake is a different story. Since the forest was never logged, there are no logging roads to follow, just a narrow path that sportsmen have been using for years. There are small blazes and signs of maintenance here and there to delineate the route, but these cannot be considered reliable markers. From the cabin site, the path skirts the western shore, crossing an outlet and a false outlet to a swampy inlet at the lake's southern corner. It would be easier to cross the ice directly to this point, but not necessary.

The path then leads south into the woods. There are few definable landmarks, just a long, gradual climb followed by a descent in stages into the Trout

Opposite: DeBraine Lake

Lake basin. You have to push through a barrier of young spruce and balsam to reach the north shore. Compared to DeBraine, Trout appears forlorn and desolate—truly a wilderness destination. Getting here entails a 1.5-mile walk from DeBraine, or 2.6 miles total from your car.

Opposite: Queer Lake Lean-to

THE WEST CENTRAL PLATEAU

On the one hand the Adirondacks are a mountainous region, and on the other they are a collection of lakes. Only in a few places are they both simultaneously.

The West Central Plateau is an area that is bounded by Piseco on the south, Indian Lake on the east, NY 28 on the north, and the private lands of the Adirondack League Club on the west. These boundaries contain the largest contiguous block of public lands in the state, consisting of the Blue Ridge and West Canada Lake wilderness areas and the Moose River Plains Wild Forest—nearly 300,000 acres of northern forest broken only by a few unplowed gravel roads.

The plateau is home to dozens of high lakes and ponds, nearly all of which are over 2000 feet. Most are rimmed with forests of balsam fir and spruce, evoking the essence of the North Country. In recent decades, moose—extirpated in the nineteenth century—have returned to the area, finding ample open space for their roamings, as well as excellent winter habitat. Deer also concentrate in areas sheltered by the dense coniferous forests, and it is a rare winter hike when you will not flush a ruffed grouse from its hiding spot under the snow.

Many miles of long trails traverse the heart of the plateau, but in the winter there is a problem with access: many of the long, gravel roads leading to the trailheads are not maintained. Therefore, excluding some extremely long treks just to reach state land, most winter snowshoe use occurs along the periphery of the area. Fortunately, there is ample state land frontage along plowed roadways, and the woods in these sections are no less wild and beautiful than in the remote wilderness core.

The plateau has always been remote and inaccessible, once attracting only a few solitary trappers who would earn their living every winter by snowshoeing through the woods to check their trap lines. The most famous of these people was Louis Seymour, who eventually built a cabin at West Lake to live in the woods permanently. Sportsmen would seek him out as a guide, and he quickly earned the nickname French Louie. His exploits in the wilderness are legendary, and his biography by Harvey Dunham is considered to be required reading by lovers of the Adirondacks.

Wilson Pond

Rating: Moderate
Round trip: 5.8 miles
Hiking time: 3 hours
Starting elevation: 1850 feet
Highest point: 2283 feet
Map: USGS Blue Mountain Lake
Who to contact: NYS DEC Northville Office

Getting there: The trailhead is a plowed turnout on the south side of NY 28, 2.8 miles from the intersection with NY 30 in Blue Mountain Lake. It is marked by a small brown sign.

This memorable little hike has a number of things going for it: a good trail, a scenic destination, and a lean-to. In addition, it passes Grassy Pond in the

At Grassy Pond

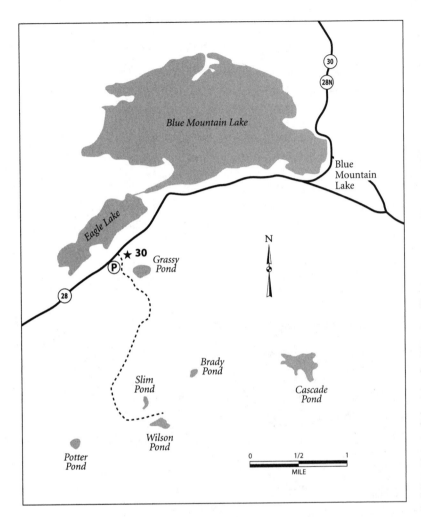

early stages of the hike, offering scenic relief at both ends of the trail. Although the trail is readily accessible from a state highway, with a parking area that is well cleared throughout the winter, Wilson Pond sees light use.

While Wilson Pond is a great destination for a moderate day trip, it is an exceptional destination for winter camping. There are a number of reasons for this, but the main factor is the lean-to. While most lean-tos face their name-sake ponds, the Wilson Pond Lean-to faces into a conifer thicket. Okay, so this is not the most scenic arrangement, but it does make this one of the most sheltered lean-tos you will find anywhere—and you will certainly appreciate it if the wind is blowing.

The trail is marked with red discs, and for the first 0.1 mile it crosses the private lands of the Eagle Nest Club to the edge of the Blue Ridge Wilderness. Shortly after crossing into state land, you reach Grassy Pond at 0.5 mile. Small and circular, it is lined by tamarack and pine. Tamaracks are conifer trees that shed all of their needles in the fall, just like the hardwoods. During the cold winter months, they appear scraggly and bare, but in fact they are quite alive. The little knobs along their twigs will sprout needles again beginning in May.

At 0.9 mile the trail cuts through the width of a long wetland, and this crossing could be impassable during a major thaw. Once back in the woods, it bears right and begins a long climb into the high country. This short distance has already put considerable distance between you and the highway. The climbing ends for the moment, and at 1.8 miles the trail fords a substantial stream—the combined outlet of three ponds.

For too short a time the trail is a narrow corridor through a lovely spruce-fir forest. Savor it. The trail then begins to make a series of sharp ups and downs as it maneuvers west of Slim Pond, although it does not pass nearly as close to Potter Pond as the USGS suggests. One final descent leads to a second stream crossing, and Wilson Pond and its lean-to are just ahead.

The trail takes you to an open ledge on the north shore of the pond, offering a vista of not only the entire pond but also of Blue Ridge Mountain in the distance. Few people venture into the wilds south of here.

--31--
Sagamore Lake Loop

Rating: Easy
Round trip: 3.9 miles
Hiking time: 2 hours
Starting elevation: 1915 feet
Highest point: 1968 feet
Map: USGS Raquette Lake
Who to contact: NYS DEC Northville Office

Getting there: There is a four-way intersection on NY 28 near the Raquette Lake School—the smallest school district in the state. Opposite the school, a large sign points south toward Great Camp Sagamore. This is a gravel road almost entirely on state land. This means that if there is a storm, it is not the top priority for plowing. Otherwise it is wide and in excellent shape. It leads to a bridge over South Inlet just over 3 miles from NY 28, and then to a second bridge a half mile later. Just before this bridge, an unplowed side road bears left, with room to park at the intersection.

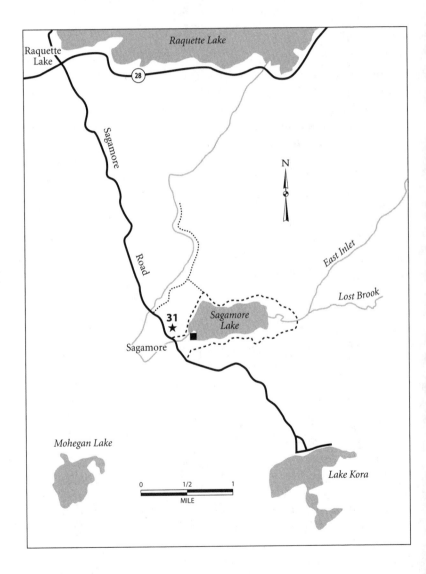

The winter trek around Sagamore Lake is more commonly used by cross-country skiers. It follows a wide carriage road over rolling terrain, with occasional views of the lake and distant mountains. However, the accessibility of this hike, along with its historical significance, makes it irresistible. It is a great easy hike in any season.

Today, Sagamore Lake is almost entirely within the state-owned Blue Ridge Wilderness. The one and only exception is Great Camp Sagamore itself, which stands prominently at the west end of the lake. Designed and constructed by William West Durant in 1897, Sagamore's first occupant was Alfred G. Vanderbilt. While considered a "camp" by the Vanderbilts perhaps, Sagamore was much more than a simple log cabin. Over the years the complex grew to a community of twenty-seven buildings for entertaining and serving guests and for housing the estate's workers.

Alfred Vanderbilt died on the *Lusitania* in 1915, and so his wife Margaret Emerson inherited the property. In 1954 she gave the property to Syracuse University, who logged the land and used the lodge as a conference center. However, the buildings deteriorated and the school sold the entire property to the state in 1973. Because the state constitution requires all state-owned lands in the Adirondack Park to be maintained as wild forest lands, a constitutional amendment was required so that the buildings could be excepted and acquired by the Sagamore Institute in 1975.

The institute does offer tours of the complex, but not in winter. The best way to enjoy the camp, then, is from the public trail that encircles the lake.

From the intersection, follow the unplowed road to the bridge over the lake's outlet. The unmarked (but obvious) trail bears left at this point to follow the north shore. It is here that you are closest to the camp. As you proceed east, the trail backs away from the shore and loops inland to a footbridge over Lost Brook at 1.9 miles. Its westward course back towards Sagamore is marked by many zigzags, and just as it approaches the buildings it bears left to stay on state land. The trail ends on Sagamore Road, and a right turn will bring you past the camp's entrance to your waiting car.

All of the forest along the route was logged in the twentieth century. However, just to the east is a large tract that was never commercially harvested (notwithstanding a salvage operation after a 1950 hurricane). There, in the valleys of East Inlet and Lost Brook, you will find virgin groves of white pines rising over a hundred feet above the ground. You have to leave the trail to find them, however.

--32--
Mohegan Lake

Rating: Moderate
Round trip: 10.4 miles
Hiking time: 5–6 hours
Starting elevation: 1791 feet
Highest point: 2224 feet
Map: USGS Raquette Lake and Wakely Mountain
Who to contact: NYS DEC Northville Office

Getting there: The trail begins across the road from the Seventh Lake boat launch, which is plowed through the winter. It is located on NY 28, 6.8 miles west of Sagamore Road and the four corners in Raquette Lake. There are rest rooms (but no running water) at the boat launch.

Mohegan Lake shares a similar history with Sagamore: it is the site of an Adirondack Great Camp, and while the building complex itself remains private, nearly all of the surrounding land has been acquired by the state. Camp Uncas

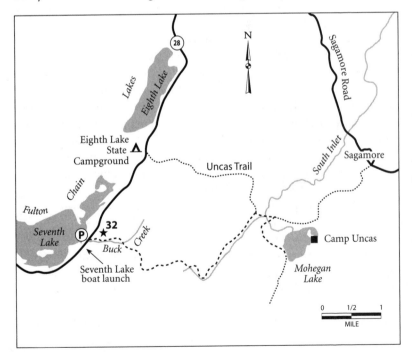

was once the wilderness retreat of J. P. Morgan, who amassed a 2750-acre preserve around the lake. The Morgan family sold the property in 1943, and thirty-two years later the state acquired all but the camp itself for the Forest Preserve. Today, what is visible of Camp Uncas from the lake hardly detracts from the wild setting.

There are actually three routes leading to Mohegan Lake, including a plowed, private road across state land that leads to a small inholding on the east shore. This would be an exceptionally easy hike, with access from Great Camp Sagamore.

Of the two trails to Mohegan Lake, the northern route—the Uncas Trail—was once the main route to Camp Uncas. It is now a wide trail, rolling across the ridges and passing a small pond along the way. It leads to the lake in 3.5 miles, and it is an excellent route for skiing.

Sheep laurel on the trail to Mohegan Lake

However, it is the southern trail that will appeal most to snowshoers. This abandoned snowmobile trail has received little maintenance in recent years, and though it is not well marked it is distinct enough that it can still be followed without much trouble. It crosses a number of frozen wetlands and passes through dense stands of snow-clad spruce, pine, and fir. The Uncas Trail is a great hike if you are looking for an easy excursion to the lake, but consider the 5.2-mile southern route if you are looking for a longer, more fulfilling day in the woods.

This route involves a 430-foot climb out of the Buck Creek drainage in the first 1.9 miles, with a few brief pitches. The forest in this section is a standard affair of northern hardwoods mixed with spruce and hemlock—but take note of them, in anticipation of the contrast to follow.

After the height-of-land, the trail passes beside a long fen with a beaver flow. The outlet of this wetland combines with several others to form a stream that will guide the trail through the valley. It is here that you enter the richly coniferous woods, with balsam and spruce crowding the trail, and tall white pine rising above. Tamarack puts in an appearance at one narrow meadow. The trail swings briefly south before making a prominent bend to the northeast, almost precisely at the same time as the stream. A large meadow just beyond is sometimes used for camping.

The long northeasterly traverse through the coniferous woods ends at the Uncas Trail intersection at 4.2 miles. A right turn here will bring you to a crossing of a wide, frozen stream in 100 yards. As you begin to rise again, red trail markers guide you to the right, off the roadway. The foot trail ends at 4.6 miles at an unplowed access road.

Although a trail sign points left, bear right and uphill on the road. This unmaintained route provides access for owners of a tiny property north of Bear Pond, and it also swings around to the western side of Mohegan Lake and is, perhaps, the best place to view the lake. Camp Uncas is hidden in the pines across the lake, with Wakely Mountain on the horizon above the eastern inlet. The scope of this view in particular gives a good sense of the vast amount of open space in this region of the Adirondack Park.

--ʒ ʒ--
Cascade Lake

Rating: Easy
Round trip: 2.6 miles
Hiking time: 2 hours
Starting elevation: 1870 feet
Highest point: 1950 feet
Map: USGS Eagle Bay
Who to contact: NYS DEC Northville Office

Getting there: From NY 28 in Eagle Bay, turn northwest onto Big Moose Road. The trailhead is a large parking area to the right at 1.4 miles.

While technically not part of the West Central Plateau, Cascade Lake and Queer Lake (Hike 34) offer a more accessible wintertime alternative to that inaccessible interior. Both are located north of Eagle Bay in the Pigeon Lake Wilderness, and the route to Cascade Lake is a popular winter trail that just about anyone can enjoy.

Like many other easy Adirondack trails, this one was once a road. In this case, it was the long driveway to a girls' camp on the lake. All of those buildings

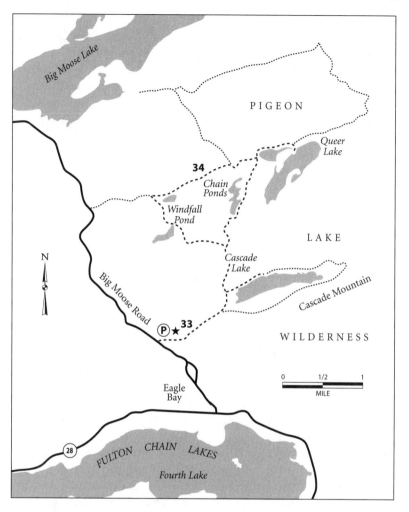

are long gone, and the entire tract is now part of the Forest Preserve, but the multi-use trail to the lake is popular in all four seasons—with hikers and equestrians in the summer, and skiers and snowshoers in the winter.

A winding foot trail leads from the parking area to the roadway, which then makes a straight line towards the lake. Just before reaching the site of the camp, at 0.8 mile, the trail forks. The way right is the return leg for the loop that completely encircles the lake, but nearly everyone bears left. An old iron post near this intersection marks the Hamilton-Herkimer county line.

The trail passes through a large clearing—site of the former camp headquarters—and then crosses the outlet on a good bridge. You pass the red-marked trail to Queer Lake (Hike 34) at 1.1 miles, and at 1.3 miles the trail reaches a large clearing on the shoreline of Cascade Lake. Many hikers go no further than this, although the trail does go all the way around the lake to make the 5-mile loop.

This clearing, as well as others further up the trail, once held the camp's dorms. In winter, the lake is an open, icebound sheet where you can search for the tracks of rabbit and deer. Although the woods were logged, a few tall pines still remain along the shore. The lake attracts skiers and snowshoers of all skill levels, and winter campers sometime build snow shelters in the old clearings.

-- 34 --
Queer Lake Loop

Rating: Moderate
Round trip: 9.7 miles
Hiking time: 6 hours
Starting elevation: 1870 feet
Highest point: 2185 feet
Map: USGS Eagle Bay
Who to contact: NYS DEC Northville Office

Getting there: From NY 28 in Eagle Bay, turn northwest onto Big Moose Road. The trailhead is a large parking area to the right at 1.4 miles.

The short trail to Cascade Lake (Hike 33) is also the start of a longer backwoods loop that visits four additional ponds. Compared with the high traffic on the trunk trail, the low use of portions of this loop imparts a deep sense of wilderness seclusion, even though it is not really that distant from the nearest roads.

The chief contributing factor to that sense of seclusion is the quality of the forest, which was never logged. When William Seward Webb was laying out the plans for his Adirondack Railroad, he had difficulty securing from the state a right-of-way through the wilderness. He therefore bought many thousands of acres—entire townships—along the proposed route. Some of this he retained for his own private preserve after the completion of the railroad, and others, such as the shoreline of Big Moose Lake, he was able to subdivide and sell.

However, some of the surplus land reverted to state ownership when Webb defaulted on the property taxes. Thus, the core of land that now forms much of the Pigeon Lake Wilderness became part of the Forest Preserve without being logged. This tract is now one of the largest, most accessible old growth forests in the Adirondacks.

There are a number of approaches to Queer Lake—a popular destination with a lean-to—but this loop is the best way to appreciate this area as a winter day trip. Begin as for Cascade Lake, but at the intersection 1.1 miles from the start, bear left onto the red-marked foot trail, which climbs out of the valley to another intersection at 1.9 miles. In this case, a blue marked trail leads right and left. Both are part of this loop, but for now bear right on the trail to Chain Ponds.

The Chain Ponds are really one long pond with a jagged outline. The

Windfall Pond outlet

trail passes close to the pond only once, shortly after crossing the small outlet stream. Afterwards, the trail parallels the shore but pulls away from it, passing through a shaded, rocky glen. It then begins to descend through a forest with large yellow birch—the largest of all the Northeastern birch species—all the way to an intersection beside Queer Lake at 3.2 miles.

Queer's name is derived from its irregular shape; a large peninsula nearly divides the lake into two separate ponds, and in a way the outline almost resembles the letter Q. The lean-to is on the far side of the peninsula, on a rock ledge with a good view. From the intersection, a yellow-marked trail leads right and curves around the bay to the lean-to. It is in good shape and well marked, but if the conditions are right it is easier to cross the ice. Either way, the lean-to should not be missed.

To complete the loop, though, you will need to bear left at the intersection. Now following yellow markers, you remain on the level for 0.25 mile, at which point the trail approaches a large cabin on an inholding of private land. The trail makes a necessary detour to the left, climbing up the side of a steep hill and then descending back towards another intersection, 0.6 mile from Queer Lake. A trail with red markers continues straight, but you should turn left.

The yellow trail next brings you to Windfall Pond. You will need to cross the outlet stream, which will likely only be a problem in a deep thaw. Just beyond the stream is another fork, and this time you will need to follow the blue trail left. It will lead you past interesting rock outcrops and an unnamed beaver pond as you close the loop. Once back at the intersection leading left to Chain Ponds, bear right on the red trail back to Cascade Lake and out to your car.

--35--
T Lake

Rating: Moderate
Round trip: 7.2 miles
Hiking time: 4 hours
Starting elevation: 1710 feet
Highest point: 2560 feet
Map: USGS Piseco Lake
Who to contact: NYS DEC Northville Office

Getting there: The trailhead is located opposite the Poplar Point State Campground on the north side of Piseco Lake. From NY 8 west of its intersection with NY 10, turn northeast onto North Shore Road and follow it for 4.2 miles. The unplowed trailhead is on the left, and the campground parking area is just beyond on the right.

The woods northwest of Piseco Lake conceal a number of high-elevation lakes, but the most accessible of them all is T Lake. Its trail begins on North Shore Road, and while the trailhead itself is not plowed, the entrance to the adjacent DEC campground is maintained for hikers and ice fishermen. The trail is not just a straight hike to the lake, but a challenging trek over mountains and through valleys. A lean-to near the lake is available for people who want to try their hand at winter camping.

    Park at the campground and cross the road to the trailhead. Following blue markers, the route begins with a long climb to a saddle at the foot of Piseco Mountain, passing through a forest filled with tall hardwoods. The major

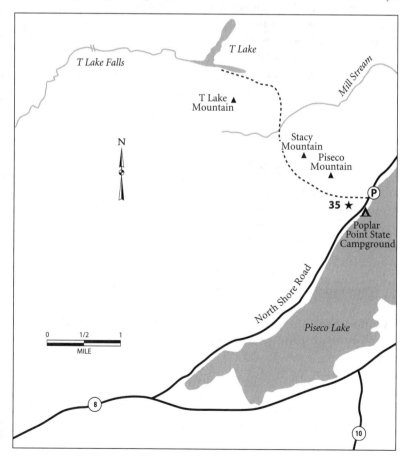

climbing ends at the saddle, but a steep descent at the far end leads into the Mill Stream valley. An icebound rock wall looms above the trail on Stacy Mountain at the top of this ascent, making one wonder whether there are any views on top. This steep descent, of course, will be a steep ascent on the return trip.

Mill Stream appears as a substantial stream, but it is usually quite solidly frozen. The trail then crosses to the foot of T Lake Mountain, making a hard left turn to angle into the T Lake fault valley. It intercepts an old woods road (the correct route should be well marked in both directions) and continues benched into the mountainside, high above the valley floor. First an open wetland appears to your right, and then the east end of the lake itself. The trail ends at 3.6 miles in a small clearing, with the lake to your right and the lean-to uphill to your left.

T Lake occupies the intersection between two fault valleys, which explains its distinctive shape. It sits on top of a plateau of hills and mountains, and its outlet takes a dramatic leap from that plateau about 2 miles away at T Lake Falls. The trail to the falls, which is still shown on topographic maps, was closed years ago because of a series of fatalities at the falls. There is a good view of the Metcalf Range from the top of the escarpment, but the rounded top of the falls and the icy rocks make T Lake Falls a dangerous place to visit in winter.

--36--
Snowy Mountain

Rating: Difficult
Round trip: 7.4 miles
Hiking time: 6 hours
Starting elevation: 1810 feet
Highest point: 3899 feet
Map: USGS Indian Lake
Who to contact: NYS DEC Northville Office

Getting there: The Snowy Mountain trailhead is located on NY 30, 17 miles north of Speculator and 7 miles south of Indian Lake. On a clear day, there are good views of the mountain from either direction along the highway.

It would be a serious omission not to include a mountain named Snowy in a snowshoeing guidebook. This particular Snowy Mountain is one of the Adirondacks' most distinctive peaks. Its profile is easily identified from other

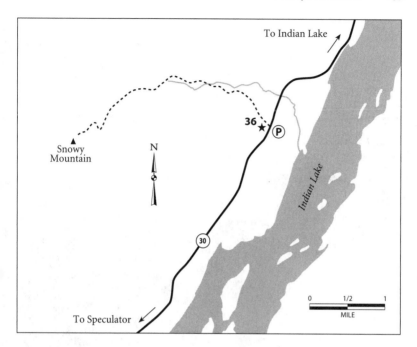

summits across the park many miles away, and at 3899 feet it is itself the high-est mountain south of Newcomb. Natural rock openings provide vistas in nearly every direction, and the fire tower completes the view with a 360-degree panorama. It is a High Peak in stature, if not in statistical fact. Therefore, as a snowshoe route it rates as difficult.

The trail begins with a minor hilly section and through-the-trees views of Squaw Mountain across the Beaver Brook valley. It crosses the brook and takes a rolling, meandering course for the first 2.5 miles, crossing Beaver Brook three more times. Take advantage of this section to "loosen up" before the big climb that begins just ahead.

The fourth crossing of Beaver Brook marks the abrupt transition from the easy walking to the difficult climb. The trail approaches this crossing level as a city street and starts uphill immediately on the other side. There will be few level places for the next 1.2 miles to the top of the mountain. Stands of spruce, fir, and birch quickly begin to fill in the forest, with some narrow places where the spruce trees grow tight to the trail.

There is a brief, level traverse, and then the trail climbs even more steeply than before. Good snow can make this second half of the climb an exciting but friendly ascent; icy conditions can make it treacherous. Since you won't know the actual conditions until you get there, you may want to have crampons on

Snowshoer appreciating the view from Snowy Mountain (Photo by Paul Kalac)

hand—the trail is worn to bedrock beneath the snow. It widens considerably on the final approach to the summit, offering views of the High Peaks before you even get to the first open ledge on the summit.

The summit views peer into the Siamese Ponds Wilderness across Indian Lake, as well as into the heart of the west central plateau to the west. From the middle landings of the tower, the view is all-inclusive. Again, the High Peaks will likely draw your attention on the northeastern horizon, but equally impressive are mountains closer in—Panther, Buell, Buck, Little Moose and Manbury, Blue Ridge (more affectionately known as Cloud Cap), and Lewey. The last two, along with Snowy itself, are part of the mountain chain known as the Little Great Range.

Allow three to four hours for the ascent, and two to three hours for the descent. It is possible to glissade down much of the distance from the summit to Beaver Brook.

--3 7--
Sucker Brook–Colvin Brook Trail

Rating: Most Difficult
Round trip: 16 miles
Hiking time: 2 days
Starting elevation: 1665 feet
Highest point: 2915 feet
Map: USGS Indian Lake
Who to contact: NYS DEC Northville Office

Getting there: The trail begins at the Lewey Lake State Campground, about 12 miles north of Speculator on NY 30. The campground roads are not plowed, but highway crews do clear the right-turn lane leading into the park, which serves as a parking area for winter hikers. Walk beside NY 30 to the north side of the bridge over Lewey's outlet, where a park road leads left to the lake. The trailhead is on this road, to the right just beyond a brown shed.

The West Canada Lake Wilderness—the largest segment of the West Central Plateau—is the second largest designated wilderness in the entire Northeast at 175,000 acres, and at its heart is a high cluster of large lakes, the West Canadas. Many miles of trails penetrate this wilderness, but of its ten trailheads, only three are located along plowed highways. The rest—including

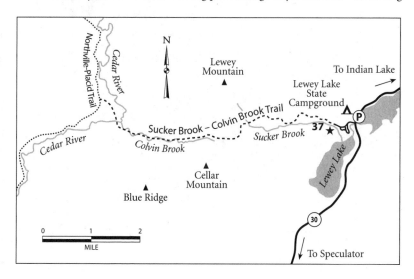

those extending to the central core of lakes—are inaccessible in winter.

The Sucker Brook–Colvin Brook Trail is the one exception, but it also happens to be the longest, most strenuous approach to the West Canada Lakes.

Relaxing at Colvin Lean-to

It begins at the Lewey Lake State Campground and strikes out west to cross a high mountain saddle, then descends through the Colvin Brook valley. The trail is notorious for its nine consecutive crossings of Colvin Brook—there is not a single bridge on the trail. It leads to a secluded lean-to on the Cedar River, where summer hikers have to ford to continue on to the lakes.

Its value for snowshoers is as a long but rewarding traverse through the mountains to Colvin Brook, where the chances for solitude are high. The forest cover throughout the hike is very fine, and in winter it is possible to see the surrounding summits. The Colvin Brook crossings are definite obstacles, of course, contributing to this trip's most difficult rating. They should only be attempted late in a very cold winter.

Because of the length of the trail and the difficult terrain, this trip is best enjoyed as a two-day camping trip. Even if the lean-to is inaccessible due to flooding, backpackers will find unlimited tent-camping opportunities along Colvin Brook. Day hikers will enjoy the walk to the saddle.

Beginning from NY 30, enter the campground and find the start of the red-marked trail, as described above. In five minutes you reach the register, where you should bear left on the foot trail. What follows for the next 3.5 miles is a long, gradual climb towards the mountain ridge. If the weather is good you will see Indian Lake behind you. Lewey Mountain (3742 feet) is the first peak to your north, with the lower flanks of Snowy beyond. The trail swings south and crosses Sucker Brook, and then begins the final steep climb to the pass. Maintenance can be poor here, so be watchful for the markers. The pass, at 3.7 miles, is frequently windy.

After a level interlude, the trail drops westward into the Colvin Brook drainage. Cellar Mountain rises to the south, with the slide-scarred summit of Blue Ridge soon peeking above Cellar's shoulder. Colvin Brook is named for Verplanck Colvin, supervisor of the first comprehensive Adirondack survey project. His name for Blue Ridge was Cloud Cap—an accurate description on many winter days, but, unfortunately, Colvin's choice did not survive to become the mountain's official name. The mountain is now one of several Blue Ridges in the Adirondack Park.

The infamous nine crossings come within the last mile of the lean-to. By this time you are hiking in a beautiful balsam forest. If the winter has been hard and the stream is frozen, then proceed with care to the lean-to. Otherwise, your current surroundings are just as beautiful, and potential winter tent sites are abundant.

My recent visits to the Colvin Brook valley have suggested that moose from the Cedar River basin have been wintering here, ranging all the way to the mountainous ridgeline. Look for their tracks and droppings in the snow.

For those snowshoers who are able to make it to the lean-to on the Cedar River, solitude is virtually guaranteed. There are exceptional views from the alder bed just downstream that look back towards Blue Ridge and the high country that you just traversed.

Opposite: View from Southerland Mountain

THE SOUTHERN ADIRONDACKS

The southern frontier of the Adirondack Park is something of a paradox. Here the mountains reach their nearest point to the Mohawk Valley, which for centuries has been one of the most settled portions of the state. Even before the modern Thruway (I-90) connected the valley's cities, the Erie Canal brought prosperity and growth. Yet, just a few miles to the north of this corridor is the Silver Lake Wilderness, the fifth largest in the Northeast and one of the least visited wild areas anywhere.

The reason for the presence of so much undeveloped land in such close proximity to civilization has to do, in a way, with the Erie Canal itself. During its heyday in the nineteenth century, the canal was the economic lifeblood of New York State. It was what connected New York City with the markets of the Midwest, giving the Port of New York an advantage that neighboring Boston and Philadelphia could not duplicate.

The state was understandably very protective of its 363-mile-long asset, which required an extensive reservoir system to keep it filled with water. When the people of the state perceived that excessive logging and the resulting forest fires were threatening the canal's major water source, the Adirondacks, the resulting political pressure was enough to convince the state legislature to take three critical actions: the establishment of the Forest Preserve in 1885; the creation of the Adirondack Park in 1892; and the passage of Article VII, Section 7, the original clause granting the preserve constitutional protection, in 1894.

The other key contributing factor to the preservation of so much open forest in the southern Adirondacks was the nature of the logging industry at the time. In the mid- to late-nineteenth century, the most economic way to get logs to the sawmills was to float them down the rivers. This limitation favored two things: the harvesting of spruce logs, which floated better than other tree species and which had high value as lumber; and the harvesting of spruce stands near water.

However, since spruce compose only a small fraction of the Adirondack forest cover, early logging operations often disturbed a correspondingly low portion of the forest. The loggers would take what spruce was accessible, float it to market, and then abandon the property. The state then generally assumed possession of these tracts due to non-payment of taxes, and they ultimately became the nucleus of the Forest Preserve.

Therefore, while other regions of the Adirondacks saw the forest clear-cut for farming, mining, and other industries, the southern Adirondacks attracted only the loggers and tanbarkers. The region quietly regrew its lost spruce trees and retained its wildness, providing outstanding recreation opportunities within easy reach of the cities of Gloversville, Johnstown, and Amsterdam.

--38--
Buckhorn Lake

Rating: Easy
Round trip: 3 miles
Hiking time: 1–2 hours
Starting elevation: 1730 feet
Highest point: 1870 feet
Map: USGS Wells
Who to contact: NYS DEC Northville Office

Getting there: The trailhead is located on NY 8 in the village of Piseco, next to the Town of Arietta highway garage. The town permits the public to park in the lot between the garage and the trail. A brown DEC sign marks the start of the trail, which is part of the Northville-Placid Trail.

Buckhorn Lake—alternately known as Fiddlers Lake—lies amidst the open hardwoods south of Piseco Lake, at the foot of a rolling ridge of hills that encircles its northern and eastern sides. Boggy shores and islands, punctuated

Buckhorn Lake

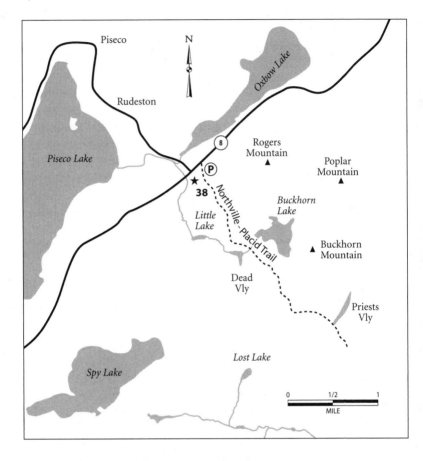

by groves of weathered snags, characterize this picturesque retreat, which is located just 0.1 mile northeast of the Northville-Placid Trail.

While located in a wilderness setting, Buckhorn is very easy to reach. The few obstacles you will encounter on the half-hour walk—a beaver-flooded stream, a brief bushwhack to get from the trail to the lake—will be enough to give you the sense that you have accomplished a rugged hike, without actually requiring you to slog for miles through the wilds. The trail is wide and obvious, and the grades are gentle. This is certainly a great hike for families.

From the town garage, follow the blue markers southeast through an overgrown clearing, across the snowmobile trail, and into deep woods. You are quickly in the wilds, putting the motorized traffic behind you. The farther you walk, the taller the hardwoods become; the bare branches of the maples, ashes, and birches rattle in the slightest breeze.

After about fifteen minutes of walking, the trail dips to cross a stream with a small beaver flow to your left. The stream fans out through the woods, and if it has not frozen you can walk across the crest of the beaver dam. Rogers Mountain rises above the snags.

The outlet of Buckhorn Lake is marked by a small, sturdy footbridge, under which the stream spills over an icy waterfall. Cross the bridge and leave the trail, turning left towards the lake. The woods are a little thicker near the water, but your own tracks will be your guide back to the trail on the return. It is possible to find a sweeping panorama from the southern shore, allowing you to take in all that Buckhorn has to offer.

Many hikers enjoy the continuing hike along the Northville-Placid Trail, walking as far as the Hamilton Lake Stream Lean-to and returning, for a total of 7.4 miles round-trip. With more hills and several stream crossings, this is a hike of moderate difficulty. Bushwhackers find little Lost Lake a challenging diversion from the trail.

--39--
Good Luck Mountain

Rating: Difficult
Round trip: 4.4 miles
Hiking time: 3 hours
Starting elevation: 1663 feet
Highest point: 2330 feet
Map: USGS Morehouse Mountain and Canada Lake
Who to contact: NYS DEC Northville Office

Getting there: The trail starts on NY 10 across from a parking turnout that is 100 yards north of a bridge over the West Branch of the Sacandaga River, and 6 miles north of the intersection of NY 10 and 29A at Pine Lake.

The ragged mountains of the northern Adirondacks do not extend into the southern Adirondack region. However, this is not to say that the south is without impressive cliffs and views. Here, a good view is often available with just a modest amount of effort, with rewards that are almost always outstanding.

Good Luck Mountain, located near Arietta, is one of the favorites of the south's climbs. The appeal lies not only in the view from the top but also in the hike that leads you there along the foot of the cliffs.

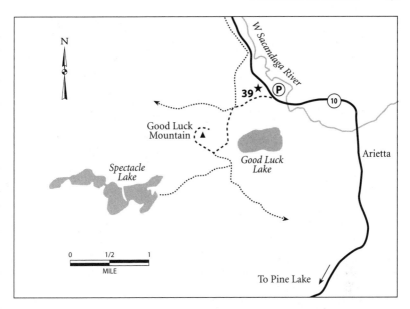

The only drawback is that Good Luck Mountain does not have a marked trail leading to its summit. However, there is an unmarked path that is used frequently enough—even in winter—that it is not too difficult to find. You do need to pay close attention to your surroundings to find your way, though.

While nearly every route in this guidebook was deliberately chosen to avoid active snowmobile trails, this trail is one case worth making an exception. Snowmobile trails in the Forest Preserve are only eight feet wide, leaving little room for passing. Since snowshoes are many times more maneuverable than snowmobiles, trail etiquette demands that walkers step off the trails when machines approach.

From the trailhead parking area on NY 10, follow the marked trail beginning across the road and to the right. At a four-way intersection, bear left towards Good Luck Lake. It is just a fifteen-minute walk past the lake, which is visible some distance downhill to your left. At this point, find and follow the footpath that begins to the right of the snowmobile trail just before it crosses a long bridge. You can now put the snowmobile trail behind you.

The path leads up the rock-filled gorge below the cliffs, which tower above you to the right. Many huge fragments have broken away from the wall, and the trail winds between some of them. After an initial climb of nearly 500 feet,

Opposite: View of Spectacle Lake from Good Luck Mountain

the route levels out briefly before hooking northeast and east for the final steep climb to the summit. The top of the cliffs is nearby on your right.

The view is primarily southwest, with a corner of Spectacle Lake just beyond the mountain. Several snowmobile trails converge on the lake, and you will likely see riders zipping across the ice. Beyond, the hills march on to the horizon, extending beyond the park boundary to the Mohawk Valley.

--40--
The County Line Lakes

Rating: Most Difficult
Round trip: 7 miles minimum
Hiking time: 6 hours minimum
Starting elevation: 1540 feet
Highest point: 2620 feet
Map: USGS Caroga Lake
Who to contact: NYS DEC Northville Office

Getting there: From Northville, follow NY 30 north for about 3 miles, where Benson Road bears left. Benson Road leads in 11.7 miles to Pinnacle Road,

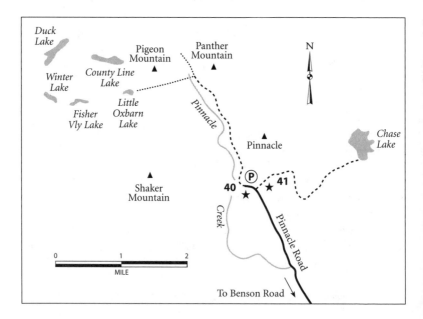

a right turn that is also marked by a sign for the Adirondack Beagle and Hare Club. Drive to the end of Pinnacle Road, 2.6 miles away.

The County Line Lakes are five small ponds tucked away in the deepest recesses of the wilderness. Ranging between 2300 and 2440 feet in elevation, they rank among the highest bodies of water in the southern region. They sit atop a plateau that receives deep snows every winter—an excellent place for snowshoeing.

Currently no trails lead to the lakes, and because they are so remote few people ever go there. Eventually, the DEC may construct a hiking trail to Little Oxbarn Lake, which will make this hike significantly easier. In the meantime, this is one of most challenging map-and-compass routes covered in this guide.

From the end of Pinnacle Road, an abandoned roadway continues straight ahead into state land. For most of its length it parallels Pinnacle

Otter tracks in the Pinnacle Creek valley

Creek. Though it has not been officially maintained for years, it has long been a popular route in all seasons. You will likely encounter skiers, or at least follow in their tracks.

The best winter route to the lakes begins by following this old trail for its entire 2.2-mile length. It will lead you through a hemlock-filled valley and past the site of a sawmill at 1.4 miles. Some people follow a flagged path to the ponds from this site, but Pinnacle Creek is often an impassable obstacle in winter. Instead, continue around the east side of a large wetland with views of Pigeon Mountain, all the way to the point where the old road seems to end deep in the woods. Allow just over an hour for this part of the journey.

At this point you will want to pick a compass course of due west. You are aiming for the saddle between Pigeon Mountain and the summit to the south, but even so you will be ascending over 700 feet. Most of the slope, all the way to the crest of the ridge, is forested with beech trees infected with the beech bark disease. About 300 feet of the climb qualifies as truly steep; make switchbacks in the snow to minimize the grade, and rotate the job of breaking trail among the members of your group.

The height-of-land is a windswept pass of stunted hardwoods, but Little Oxbarn Lake is just ahead, at the foot of the ridge. Shaped like an apostrophe, it is surrounded by an open hardwood forest that is no doubt kept clear by the beavers. It takes well over an hour to reach it from the Pinnacle Creek trail.

Strong, ambitious hikers could theoretically make a long loop that visits all five of the lakes, but it took me two separate visits to reach them all. Each lake has its own distinct quality. Winter Lake is nestled within a deep basin of snow-clad spruce, while Fisher Vly Lake is a small pond contained within a larger wetland. Next to Duck Lake is an icy waterfall on the outlet stream of County Line Lake. Navigating between the lakes is not always easy, but it represents Adirondack bushwhacking at its best.

After you visit the isolated lakes and return to the Pinnacle Creek trail, the handful of snowshoers and skiers that use that old road will make it seem like a superhighway by comparison.

--41--
Chase Lake

Rating: Moderate
Round trip: 5.2 miles
Hiking time: 2–3 hours
Starting elevation: 1540 feet
Highest point: 1580 feet
Map: USGS Caroga Lake and Jackson summit
Who to contact: NYS DEC Northville Office

Getting there: From Northville, follow NY 30 north for about 3 miles, where Benson Road bears left. Benson Road leads in 11.7 miles to Pinnacle Road, a right turn that is also marked by a sign for the Adirondack Beagle and Hare Club. Drive to the end of Pinnacle Road, 2.6 miles away.

From the same starting point as the demanding route to the County Line Lakes (Hike 40), a marked trail leads east on a much different journey to a little-visited lake. With its lean-to, easy trail, and fine views of the Pinnacle, Chase Lake would seem to have all the ingredients of a popular destination. Nevertheless, the

DEC reports that an average of a hundred people visit the lake each year.

The trail was once used by snowmobiles, but today the few people who do go to Chase Lake do so under their own power. The DEC has proposed to re-designate the trail for foot travel only, as well as to replace the old lean-to with a new one on the more scenic eastern shoreline.

Woods near Chase Lake

From the end of Pinnacle Road, follow the marked trail that leads off to the right. The trail was designed to circumvent private land. It essentially parallels the boundary, leading north of east around a knoll, and then cutting southeast through a deep ravine. Beyond, you are so close to the private parcel that you can clearly see the difference between the cut-over forest and the mature stand on state land.

After walking for 1 mile, you intercept the original trail and bear left to follow it. You are now on what appears to be an old woods road, following beside a wide draw that is unusual in its straight course and unchanging dimensions. Indeed much of the remaining hike to the lake passes through level terrain—a rare pause in the mountainous Adirondack landscape. The trail circles and dips to cross a low swampy area, and then resumes its east-northeast course to the lean-to near the south end of the lake.

The current lean-to site is not particularly well suited to allow its guests to consider the scenic charms of Chase Lake, and no doubt this is why it leaves a bland impression with so many of its visitors. If and when DEC extends the trail around the southern corner of the lake to the proposed new shelter on the east shore, then more people might take note. While the western shore is hemmed in with extensive marshlands, the eastern shore has a number of rocky points, each one capped with a scenic tent site. They are in a prime position to take in the view of the Pinnacle, with the reddish-colored cliffs draped across the northern shoulder of the mountain. For the few people who take the time to cross to this shore in winter, Chase Lake takes on a whole new dynamic.

A trip to Chase Lake can be combined with the off-trail treks to Mud Lake and along the spine of the Pinnacle—adventures sure to attract the skilled backwoods navigator.

--42--
Groff Creek

Rating: Moderate
Round trip: 4.4 miles
Hiking time: 2–3 hours
Starting elevation: 925 feet
Highest point: 1375 feet
Map: USGS Three Ponds Mountain
Who to contact: NYS DEC Northville Office

Getting there: From Northville, follow NY 30 north for about 3 miles,

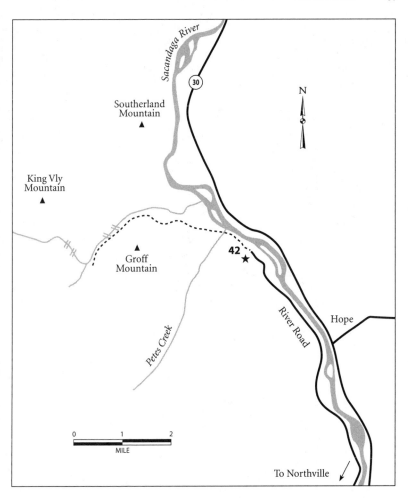

then bear left onto Benson Road. River Road then turns right almost immediately. Follow it to its end, where it narrows into a rough track, and where a sign indicates that the remaining public highway has been abandoned by the town. There is room for a few cars to park. (Note that sometimes in late March the town barricades the road at a point nearly 2 miles south of here to protect it during the spring frost-out.)

One of my favorite corners of the southern Adirondacks is Groff Creek, a secluded stream that flows through a deep-cut valley between Groff and Southerland mountains. It is located west of the Sacandaga River, and while this part

of the park is not known for copious amounts of snowfall, the Groff Creek valley sees little direct sunlight and therefore retains snow a little longer than its immediate surroundings.

More to the point, though, is the fact that this is a great woodland walk for snowshoers who revel in secluded wilderness nooks. It is one of my favorites, actually. What draws me to Groff Creek is the richness of the surrounding mixed woods, which abound with eastern hemlock (and to a lesser degree red spruce). There are few things more beautiful than a hemlock stand on a sunny winter day, when the boughs and twigs strain the light to cast intricate shadows on the snow.

The valley is accessed by an unmarked footpath, which over a century ago was a major logging road. It originally led beyond Groff Creek to a lumber camp and dam at Devorse Creek, from which additional logging roads branched out all throughout the backcountry. Only the first 2.2 miles of that road still survive, the rest having been reclaimed by the wilderness long ago.

This route begins along the abandoned highway, which is still a public right-of-way across private land. From the end of the plowed road, set off on foot up the unplowed/unmaintained section northwest, passing a cinderblock camp beside Petes Creek. At a major fork just beyond the bridge, bear right onto the rougher road. A few minutes more brings you to the Forest Preserve boundary, beyond which the route narrows into an attractive footpath.

A level section leads you west to the foot of Groff Mountain, followed by a quick ascent that brings you into the deep valley. Your first sight of Groff Creek is through the hemlock boles far below you. The mountainside both above and below you is quite steep, but the path is benched into the slope and climbs gradually.

After passing high above two small waterfalls, the valley begins to open up, allowing the stream and the trail to approach the same level. Just then, however, Groff Creek makes a major bend to the northwest. The path pulls beside a tributary instead and comes to a stop beside a small beaver flow. The roadbed once continued to Devorse Creek, but today that section exists only on old USGS maps.

There are two other waterfalls just upstream from the elbow bend on Groff Creek. You will need to cross the beaver dam to get to them. One of the most beautiful mixed stands of red spruce and hemlock grows here, shading the falls and competing with their beauty. The taller of the two cascades is only eight feet high, but the secluded setting is perfect. A narrow, rocky trough connects the two falls, which are often icy ledges in winter.

Opposite: Frozen waterfall on Groff Creek

--43--
Vly Creek and Southerland Mountain

Rating: Most Difficult
Round trip: 6 miles minimum
Hiking time: 6 hours
Starting elevation: 1005 feet
Highest point: 1811 feet
Map: USGS Three Ponds Mountain
Who to contact: NYS DEC Northville Office

Getting there: From NY 30 in Wells, turn west onto Algonquin Drive beside the dam on Lake Algonquin. Then turn left onto West River Road at 0.7 mile, and continue southwest to Blackbridge at 2.4 miles. Turn left to cross the bridge over the West Branch of the Sacandaga River and immediately bear left again on Hernandez Road. Follow this road to its end, which is a wide turnaround area.

While there are many miles of trail in New York, it is also important to forego all trails every once and a while and simply plot your own course through the woods. The southern Adirondacks provide abundant opportunities for the wil-

View from Southerland Mountain

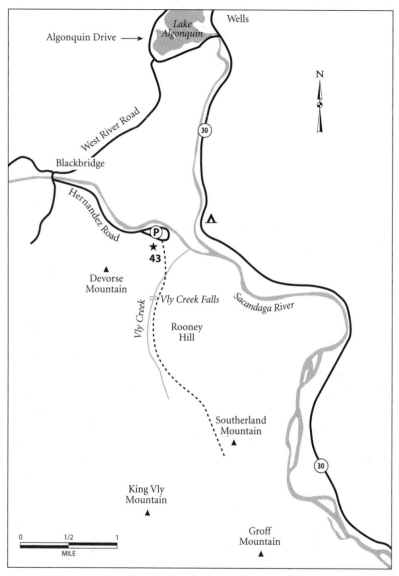

derness explorer to penetrate into nooks and crannies where few people ever go. Winter is an especially good time for this kind of travel, when snow blankets the underbrush and ice solidifies the running streams.

Here is a trailless route that offers several highlights: a secluded stream valley, a waterfall, an open wetland, and a small mountain with an open view. While there are easier ways to get to the Southerland Mountain, this route from the north makes for a more substantial day in the woods.

From the end of plowing on Hernandez Road, two unplowed forks continue into state land. This was a property that the state purchased in 1964, and the two forks form a short loop. Begin on the right fork, and follow it for 0.15 mile to a small sand pit. Look for a narrow footpath branching off to the right, into deep woods. You may be able to follow it for a short distance to a log bridge across Vly Creek.

This route will take you up Vly Creek to its headwaters, and the best walking conditions are found on the east bank. Cross the creek on the logs, or else find some other way across, and then parallel the stream as you head south. You may find a path benched into the hillside set back from the stream, and the walking is certainly easiest here.

Twenty minutes from the start, you reach Vly Creek Falls. It is located within a narrow gorge, but its orientation is unusual in that rather than flowing over a headwall, the stream sneaks around to spill into the gorge from the side. It is not a completely vertical cascade, but the total drop is some thirty or forty feet. With care it is possible to descend the bank for a close view.

The valley opens up considerably above the falls, and it is forested with rich hemlock stands. Follow the creek's east bank, ultimately reaching the large vly, or open wetland, that gives the creek its name. Here the weathered remains of dozens of white pines stand guard around the meadow, permitting views of the surrounding mountains and ridges. From this vantage, Southerland appears as a series of steep-sided, spruce-covered peaks to the southeast.

The best views on Southerland Mountain are found on the southernmost of its three summits, and the best approach is to circle around the east side of the vly and pass below the foot of the northern slopes. A small stream drains the notch between the middle and southern summits, and this is also a good place to climb the mountain. Hemlock crowns the southern summit; look for the wide-open ledges along the southern face.

The Groff Creek valley (Hike 42) is clearly defined before you, and with the aid of a map you can easily identify Groff Mountain, Cathead Mountain with its fire tower, Wallace and Three Ponds mountains at the head of Devorse Creek, and King Vly Mountain. A corner of Great Sacandaga Lake is also visible. A smaller ledge to the northwest extends the view back toward Vly Creek and Finch Mountain.

There may well be other views elsewhere on the middle summit, and if you have allowed yourself plenty of time you will be able to vary your return route by following the ridgeline north before descending toward Vly Creek.

Opposite: Crossing the suspension bridge over the East Branch Sacandaga River

THE SIAMESE PONDS WILDERNESS

The Siamese Ponds lie at the heart of New York's fourth largest wilderness. However, unlike the West Canada Lake Wilderness to the west, access to this tract is nearly as good in winter as it is in summer. It is crisscrossed by a network of long trails, most of which were laid out along the routes of nineteenth-century roadways. This makes the area attractive to cross-country skiers and snowshoers alike.

The region survives as a truly wild area today, but in the nineteenth century a number of people attempted to tame the land and harness its resources in a number of different ways. Lumbermen, of course, built their camps and dammed the rivers to control the flow of water for spring log drives. Tanneries depended on the supply of hemlock found in the interior. Farmers cleared small fields and even attempted to establish a settlement deep in the interior. Several of today's hiking routes were once the main travel corridors between communities.

Today you may well find stone foundations of the dams, the mills, and the farmhouses, but you will be impressed at how little of a long-term impact these aborted human enterprises have had on the wilderness resource. This was a brief eye-blink in the long history of the land. The most enduring reminders of that period will be the names those early visitors bestowed on the ponds and the mountains.

--44--
Siamese Ponds from Eleventh Mountain

Rating: Moderate
Round trip: 13.2 miles
Hiking time: 7 hours
Starting elevation: 1772 feet
Highest point: 2165 feet
Map: USGS Bakers Mills
Who to contact: NYS DEC Warrensburg Office

Getting there: The Eleventh Mountain Trailhead is on NY 8 between Wells and Wevertown. From Wells, it is 13.5 miles northeast from the intersection with NY 30 north of the village, near the bridge over the Sacandaga River. From Wevertown, drive west on NY 8 through Bakers Mills, and continue 4 miles more to the trailhead. There is a large parking area that is well-maintained through the winter, marked by brown DEC signs.

This trail is the main artery into the Siamese Ponds Wilderness, and the primary route to the ponds themselves. Since such a long stretch of the walk is close to the East Branch of the Sacandaga River, the 6.6-mile walk is quite scenic. The portion along the river is a classic ski route, but the portion of the trail across the shoulder of Eleventh Mountain—with its patches of bare ice and the long descent into the East Branch valley—puts snowshoers at an advantage over skiers. The biggest challenge for snowshoers will be the return climb over Eleventh Mountain.

Marked with blue disks, the trail leads away from the highway as it circles around the steep southwestern face of the mountain. There is some brief climbing towards a height-of-land, where a stream flowing over the trail is often glare ice. Then the long descent begins, leading to a footbridge over Diamond Brook at 1.5 miles. This 400-foot descent will be a 400-foot ascent at the end of the day.

Diamond Brook, at 1607 feet, represents the lowest point along the hike. By now you have begun to glimpse the East Branch through the trees to your left. The trail will draw very close to the river at several points, but it is often worthwhile to step off the trail to a steal a glimpse of some of the outward bends. As the river freezes and thaws, it can heave giant blocks of ice onto its banks. The East Branch, with its deep and powerful flow, rarely freezes enough for hikers to cross it. Destinations that lie across the river, such as Curtis Clearing, should be considered off limits during winter.

At 2.5 miles you pass through Burnt Shanty Clearing, which is now filled in with a young forest and a gnarled apple tree or two. You continue close to the

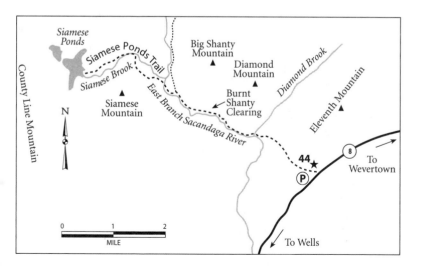

Trail beside the East Branch Sacandaga River

river, and at 3.7 miles there is a fork. Bear left, which is the 0.5-mile connector to the Sacandaga Lean-to and the large suspension bridge over the river.

The bridge seems to be overdone in this wilderness setting, but it was built before the wilderness classification and therefore has been grandfathered in. You will need it to get to the Siamese Ponds trail. This section sees somewhat less use. The trail immediately leads away from the river, following instead the ponds' outlet stream. There is an icy crossing of that stream, and then a long, 300-foot climb up to the ponds, ending 2.5 miles from the bridge on the east side of the lower pond.

The ponds are not now conjoined, although they may have been in the past when the stone dam on the outlet was still intact. Today, the only way to see the smaller pond is to cross the lower one. White birches march down to the shoreline, and the multisummitted County Line Mountain looms like a broken ridgeline to the west. If you do decide to add to your day's adventures the trek across or around the pond, bear in mind the long hike back to your car, and especially the climb over the shoulder of Eleventh Mountain.

--*45*--

Puffer Pond and Twin Ponds

Rating: Difficult
Round trip: 6.5 miles
Hiking time: 6 hours
Starting elevation: 1735 feet
Highest point: 2360 feet
Map: USGS Thirteenth Lake
Who to contact: NYS DEC Warrensburg Office

Getting there: The Kings Flow Trailhead accesses this corner of the Siamese Ponds Wilderness. It is located at the very end of Big Brook Road, which turns off of NY 30 at the south end of Indian Lake village. The public parking area is located in a private development, and there is a modest parking fee of $2 per car per day.

Puffer Pond in itself would be a fairly easy destination to reach, with some moderate climbing along the way and an attractive lean-to for a winter overnight trip. However, for snowshoers who are really looking to delve into the

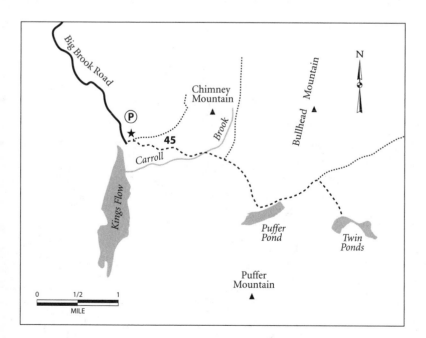

heart of the wilderness, Puffer Pond will be just a scenic waypoint on a longer, more difficult winter trek. Twin Ponds, several miles to the east of Puffer, is a beautiful and secluded destination for winter camping.

At the trailhead parking area, the trail to Chimney Mountain forks left, and the red-marked trail to Puffer Pond bears right. The trail enters state land just minutes from the start, and then approaches Carroll Brook. The trail crosses the brook in a beaver meadow—there is no bridge. This may not be an obstacle in midwinter, but I can personally attest that the crossing is impassable when it thaws. I once found myself cut off during an April snowshoe trip when this brook, which was nicely frozen over Friday evening, became a raging torrent by Sunday afternoon when the temperature rose to 60°F.

The trail pulls away from Carroll Brook, passes the blue-marked trail to John Pond, and then begins to climb 400 feet to a height-of-land. A 200-foot descent follows, ending at the lean-to on the north side of Puffer Pond, 2 miles from the trailhead. The DEC reconstructed this shelter in 2005, and while it is set back from the shore, this spot is poised to take in the sweep of Puffer Mountain to the south.

Bear left on the marked trail, which follows the shoreline for another 0.5 mile to the eastern lean-to. (This one is slated for removal.) The trail continues east away from the pond, leading ultimately to the Old Farm Trailhead. Follow it for another ten minutes or so from the pond, as it continues on the level. Where it crosses a small stream and rises beside some large glacial erratics, look for old blazes or other markings on the trees beside the trail. They are all that mark the beginning of the informal path to Twin Ponds, which in winter can be a difficult route to follow. It will certainly test your route-finding skills.

Basically the path follows a course just south of east through a notch in a ridge, descending to a designated campsite beside the western pond. The route may be marked with additional small blazes, or hatchet cuts made into the barks of trees. This is a traditional way to mark trails in the Adirondacks, although it can impact the health of the tree and is therefore illegal. Twin Ponds is an hour's walk from Puffer Pond, and if you cannot find the path be prepared to bushwhack.

Twin Ponds is screened by a barrier of trees, but from a point nearby on the shore there is a great view up to the frosty heights of Puffer Mountain. A long and high set of cliffs on that mountain are just around a corner of the peak, and therefore tantalizingly out of view. Twin Ponds makes a great base camp for deeper explorations of the wilderness—the area south of here is not well known at all.

Opposite: View of Puffer Mountain from inside the Puffer Pond Lean-to

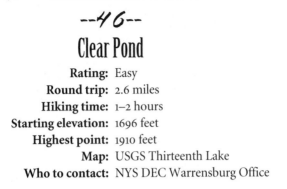

--46--
Clear Pond

Rating: Easy
Round trip: 2.6 miles
Hiking time: 1–2 hours
Starting elevation: 1696 feet
Highest point: 1910 feet
Map: USGS Thirteenth Lake
Who to contact: NYS DEC Warrensburg Office

Getting there: From NY 30 at the south end of Indian Lake village, turn onto Big Brook Road. Follow it for 1.8 miles to Starbuck Road, a left turn.

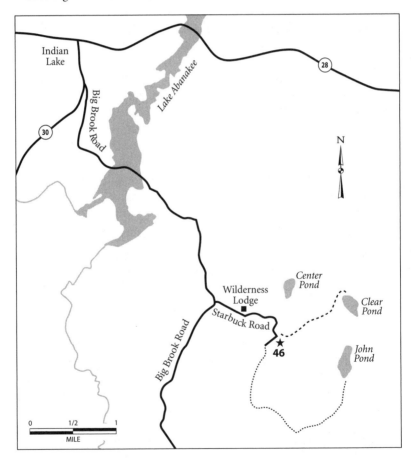

Outlet of Clear Pond

There is a T intersection 1.2 miles later, where you will find the start of the trail. The only parking available is at roadside.

The trail to Clear Pond begins on the edge of a residential area and leads in a short distance to a pond surrounded by white birch. It is a modest hike with minor elevation change and a handsome destination. The start of this route is just a short drive outside of Indian Lake, where you will find supplies, accommodations, and other small-town services.

The red-marked trail begins on the side of the road, skirting around the last cluster of camps before striking a course straight for the pond. A few small streams break up the terrain, which is otherwise marked by the slopes of John Pond Ridge to your right and a lowland valley to your left. The mixed-woods forest is beautiful.

Over thirty minutes from your car, the trail passes through a blowdown area and approaches the outlet of the pond. This small stream may have several channels as a result of beaver flooding, but once across, the trail ends in a short distance at a campsite at the north end of the pond.

The white birch forest is a clear indication that this area was ravaged by a forest fire, for these trees require a lot of sunlight and could not become established in the shade of other trees. The blowdown has opened the forest again, and you can already get a taste for what the next stand will consist of by the saplings that have established a foothold among the fallen trees.

--47--
Extract Brook

Rating: Difficult
Round trip: 4.6 miles
Hiking time: 3 hours
Starting elevation: 1260 feet
Highest point: 1715 feet
Map: USGS Harrisburg and Bakers Mills
Who to contact: NYS DEC Warrensburg Office

Getting there: From the NY 8/30 intersection north of Wells, follow NY 8 east for 2.5 miles, where a narrow dirt road turns left. It is not always easy to spot, but it is plowed and it leads to the only highway bridge across

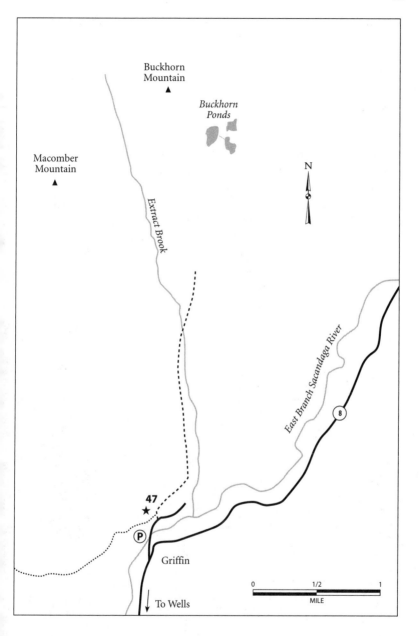

the entire East Branch of the Sacandaga River, at Griffin. Park in the widening just beyond the bridge, in the crotch where an unplowed road bears left and the plowed road bears right.

The East Branch of the Sacandaga River is the primary stream draining the eastern edge of the wilderness, and for several miles, where it runs parallel to NY 8, the river literally forms the wilderness boundary. The drive through its valley is among the most scenic in the Adirondacks, especially in winter when the view is not obstructed by leaves. Several rugged mountains stand guard over the opposite bank, many with open ledges that in theory would be excellent snowshoe-bushwhack destinations.

The drawback is the river itself, which is spanned by only one highway bridge in its entire length—the narrow little truss at Griffin. Since crossing the river directly on the ice is a risky proposition even in the best of times, the Griffin bridge takes on a strategic importance for snowshoers looking to explore the portion of the Siamese Ponds Wilderness west of the river. The best hike from the bridge is the informal path alongside Extract Brook.

Buckhorn Mountain from the Extract Brook valley

The difficulty in this hike lies in the fact that it is not a marked trail. However, it follows an unmarked path that leads into a wild valley, with the potential to be the springboard for a number of off-trail adventures. The path follows an old woods road north along the brook and ends eventually at a beaver flow. Its history is rooted in the tanning industry, and indeed this entire hike might be considered an historical exploration.

Leather tanneries were once quite numerous in the Adirondacks. A chemical found in the bark of hemlock trees, tannin, was a key ingredient for the leather-curing process, and in the nineteenth century it was more economical to ship hides from all across the hemisphere to these tanneries in the wilds than it was to get the tannin closer to the source of the hides.

Small communities developed around the mills, and roads led into the forest to access the hemlock stands. Tanbarkers harvested the trees in massive numbers, although the only part required in the tanning process was the bark. Then, after just a few decades, the tanneries all closed. In many cases, the communities surrounding them faded from existence as well. Here in Griffin, a small collection of camps occupies part of the site, but the rest of the site—including the foundations of the tannery itself—lies on what is now reforested state land.

The beginning of the path is on private land, and so without permission to cross from the landowner you will need to take a short detour. From the fork at the far end of the bridge in Griffin, head into the woods between the two roads and bear right to follow the foot of the knoll. You may well spot some of the foundations through the snow. The yellow-blazed state land boundary passes nearby, marked as paint daubs on a line of trees. Follow the boundary north of east for 0.4 mile to the point where it crosses the path, which should appear wide and obvious.

For the first mile or so the path stays well out of sight of Extract Brook, although it will swing quite close later on. Despite the history of this valley, there is no shortage of hemlocks here today. A number of trees have grown quite large. At over 2 miles from the start, the path crosses the brook, which could be an obstacle if not frozen. Look for a suitable ice bridge or a stable fallen log.

Now on the east side of the stream, the path pulls away from Extract Brook as it climbs gradually up the side of a knoll. Again, hemlocks tower above the snow, leaving little doubt as to what attracted the tanbarkers to this valley. The route ends at 2.3 miles, beside a large beaver flow, with Buckhorn Mountain looming above.

The walk to this point is a secluded and peaceful wilderness trip in itself, but for the adventurous it can be extended in several ways. I have used this path as the jumping off point for the bushwhack to the Buckhorn Ponds, located high up on their namesake mountain. The dense forest between the ponds makes getting about the high country rather challenging. A somewhat easier trek is the walk to the source of Extract Brook: a deep notch between Buckhorn and Macomber mountains. Either trip makes for a full winter's day.

Opposite: Black Dome from Blackhead

THE NORTHERN CATSKILLS

In comparing the Catskill Mountains to the Canadian Rockies, the travelogue writer T. Morris Longstreth commented: "There is nothing big about the Catskills. They are as comfortable as home. They were created, not for observation-cars, but for bungalow porches." Lacking dramatic rock faces—or even peaks, for that matter—the Catskills were not the kind of over-the-top scenery that drew people from half a continent away to come and gawk at them. Rather, these mountains with their rounded contours were something that offered comfort and pleasure, while retaining their wildness.

Indeed, many people still find pleasure living within the broad valleys of the northern Catskills, with the rounded mountains as neighbors. This is the most heavily developed portion of the Catskill Park, crisscrossed by good roads and populated by dozens of small towns. The latter range in character from the artists' colony known as Woodstock to the ski center known as Hunter, with picturesque places like Phoenicia thrown in for good measure.

From a snowshoer's perspective, the northern Catskills feature two highlights: the Escarpment and the Devils Path Mountains. The former is perhaps one of the most iconic features of the Catskill landscape, where the mountains begin abruptly by rising 3000 feet above the lowlands of the Hudson Valley. In geological terms, the Escarpment is the ultimate manifestation of the Catskills' origins as the upended bed of a Devonian sea. Nearly all of the Escarpment has been placed under the protection of the Forest Preserve, and indeed this narrow ridge is one of the most unusual places for snowshoeing covered in this guide.

The Devils Path Mountains, on the other hand, represent the Catskills at their most rugged. The Devils Path is an aptly named 30-mile trail that traces a course up, over, and down some of the steepest slopes in the park. Although they are not terribly large, these are not mountains to be scoffed at. In fact, many of these mountains tend to be difficult climbs. Ice build-up on the rocky slopes makes the trails too dangerous in some places for novice snowshoers. Therefore, I have selected only one trail in this range—Hunter Mountain—to give a taste of what snowshoeing here can be like.

Indeed, the snowshoe routes in the northern Catskills are among the most diverse and memorable anywhere in the Northeast.

The region is eminently accessible, being traversed by three principle east-west highways—NY 23, 23A, and 28—and many good secondary highways. The Thruway (I-87) even passes within view of the Escarpment near Catskill.

--48--
Sunset Rock and Inspiration Point

Rating: Easy
Round trip: 3 miles
Hiking time: 1–2 hours
Starting elevation: 2240 feet
Highest point: 2260 feet
Map: USGS Kaaterskill
Who to contact: NYS DEC Stamford Office

Getting there: From NY 23A in Tannersville, turn onto North Lake Road (CR 18). At 2.2 miles, just before the campground entrance, turn right onto Schutt Road (sometimes Scutt Road). The trailhead parking area is on the right at 0.1 mile.

The North/South Lake State Campground is one of the most popular recreational areas in the Catskills. It is surrounded by an overlapping network of

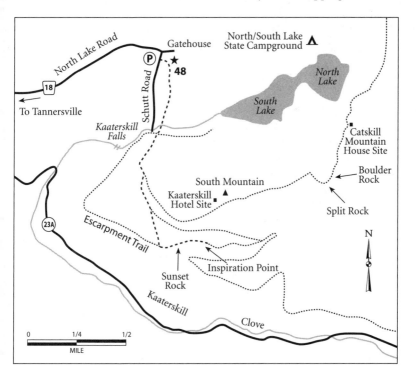

Ice-covered ledge at Inspiration Point

trails and old roads, all of them suited for short day trips. In fact there are so many destinations within easy reach that it is hard to settle on just one.

At the same time, if hiking here has one difficulty it is in navigating one's way through the various trail intersections. Fortunately, there are plenty of signs to lead the way, and since many of the trails follow old carriage roads, the snowshoeing is very easy.

For this guide, I selected for a destination a point on the Escarpment overlooking the Kaaterskill Clove. It offers all of the advantages of a lofty mountain view, but without much of a climb to get there. The clove is a deep canyon etched into the side of the mountain plateau, with Kaaterskill High Peak (once believed to be the highest mountain in the state) rising in profile to the south. Except for the moderate traffic on NY 23A below, the scene is peaceful and wild.

This area was the realm of the Kaaterskill and Catskill mountain houses, and the Laurel House at the top of the famed Kaaterskill Falls is also nearby. All of these sites are now in the Forest Preserve.

The trail begins across from the parking area on Schutt Road, following blue markers. It turns south to parallel the road, passing through a beautiful forest with many tall white pines. The first half mile of walking is very busy; the pair of footbridges and the pair of abandoned railroad grades that the trail crosses may leave you with a strong feeling of déjà vu.

At 0.5 mile, after crossing the second footbridge, you reach a major intersection. Continue straight on a wide old roadbed, now following red markers. In another 0.25 mile, turn right onto another roadway, this one marked with yellow disks. The roads offer easy snowshoeing through the mixed woods. Then, after about 1 mile of walking overall, another trail sign points right for Sunset Rock and Inspiration Point. This 0.2-mile foot trail connects with the blue-marked Escarpment Trail, and both Sunset Rock and Inspiration Point are a short distance to the left.

With their south-facing orientation, these ledges receive a lot of direct sunlight and may not always be snow-covered; take care with patches of ice around Inspiration Point. Both offer outstanding views of the clove, and of the streams that drop precipitously off Kaaterskill High Peak. What is great about this hike is that it only takes forty-five minutes or so to reach this rugged spot.

--49--
Blackhead Mountain Loop

Rating: Most Difficult
Round trip: 5.2 miles
Hiking time: 4 hours
Starting elevation: 2140 feet
Highest point: 3940 feet
Map: USGS Freehold
Who to contact: NYS DEC Stamford Office

Getting there: To find the trailhead from NY 296 in Hensonville, turn onto CR 40. In 2 miles you reach Maplecrest. Here, bear left onto CR 56, or Big Hollow Road, which you should follow for 4 miles to the end of winter plowing. There is room here to park, but avoid the portion reserved as a snowplow turnaround.

From neighboring mountains, Blackhead is a lump of a mountain with a rounded top and steep sides. It is connected to but somewhat apart from Black Dome Mountain, and while it is part of the Escarpment, it towers above every

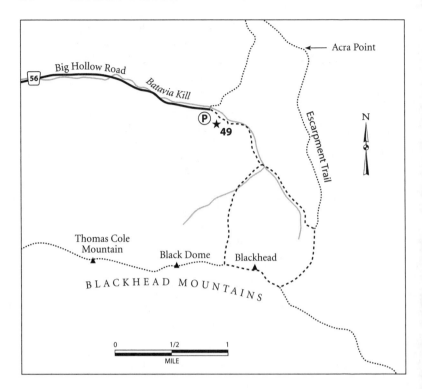

other knob on that mountain wall. In fact, it is higher than most other Catskill peaks—at 3940 feet, it is the fourth highest in the park.

As a winter snowshoe hike, the steep mountainsides present a formidable obstacle no matter which of the three trails you take to or from the summit. The rock ledges along the trail are certain to have patches of ice under the snow. But if you take your time and make sure to maintain three points of contact with the mountain at all times as you climb, you will find Blackhead to be among the most rewarding climbs in the Catskills.

A very good loop hike up and over the mountain is available from the end of Big Hollow Road. Indeed, since Blackhead is one of the four required winter climbs for membership in the Catskill 3500 Club (for people who have climbed all thirty-five Catskill High Peaks over 3500 feet), this is a popular climb, despite its difficulties. It leads up the mountain's steepest slope, which is more safely taken as an ascent rather than a descent. While the route down the mountain is also steep, it is possible to glissade, or slide on your snowshoes, down this slope because of its straighter, more open course.

Setting off on foot, you pass the summer parking area at 0.1 mile and a footbridge over the Batavia Kill just beyond. Follow the red markers as it follows the kill upstream, and then bear left at the intersection with a yellow trail. The red trail on your right will be your return route. After forty-five minutes you reach the Batavia Kill Lean-to; the curious pattern carved into its floor are teeth marks made by porcupines, who are prodigious gnawers.

It is a gentle, switchbacking route out of the Batavia Kill drainage to the crest of the Escarpment, which you reach in one hour. Bear right on the blue-marked Escarpment Trail for the ascent to Blackhead—an ascent that begins right at the intersection. A sharp climb through a rocky defile brings you to your first view of the day, this one overlooking the lowlands sprawling beyond

Trail intersection near Blackhead Mountain

the park's boundary. Downtown Albany is easy to spot on a clear day.

Blackhead's summit looms above the bare treetops, and its steepness is no illusion. Before long you are meeting the mountain face-to-face, slowly working your way up the various ledges. The way is so twisty and steep that you will be glad to be going down the mountain on a different trail. Do not hurry. It is a beautiful mountain, and there are frequent views through the trees of the sprawling countryside.

You reach the summit at 2.5 miles, and at least two hours from your car. Spruce and balsam grow thickly here. The trail splits, with the yellow trail to the right being your route back. However, take a moment to see the view on the left fork just 0.1 mile away, overlooking the Hudson Valley and Cairo Roundtop.

The yellow trail traverses the balsam-capped summit to another scenic ledge, this one peering into the heart of the Catskills. Hunter is a prominent landmark by virtue of its ski slopes, and Plateau, Sugarloaf, Twin, and Indian Head are also visible to its left. Black Dome looms above the continuing trail, which now sends you sliding into a deep col between the two peaks. You reach an intersection 0.6 mile from the summit, where now you want to bear right for the final pitch down into the Batavia Kill basin. A very pleasant mixed woods shelters these slopes. A left turn at the foot of the mountain, beside the stream, closes your loop and returns you to your car. In about four hours of snowshoeing you will have covered 5.2 miles of steep terrain—not a bad way to spend the day!

--*50*--
Windham High Peak

Rating: Moderate
Round trip: 6.6 miles
Hiking time: 3–4 hours
Starting elevation: 2060 feet
Highest point: 3524 feet
Map: USGS Hensonville, Freehold
Who to contact: NYS DEC Stamford Office

Getting there: The trailhead at the end of Peck Road provides the shortest approach to the summit. From NY 296 in Hensonville, turn onto CR 40 towards Maplecrest, which you reach in 2 miles. Here, bear left onto CR 56, or Big Hollow Road, and follow it for 1.8 miles to Peck Road, another left turn. Follow Peck Road to its end, where you will find the trailhead parking area.

At 3524 feet in elevation, Windham is one of the less conspicuous of the thirty-five Catskill High Peaks, especially when viewed from the neighboring Blackhead Range; but its position along the Escarpment gives it a dramatic profile above NY 23. There are three trailheads and two approaches to the summit of Windham High Peak, with either of the approaches from the west being among the most moderate mountain climbs in the Catskill region.

In fact the mountain's western face is so gently sloped that at one time farm pastures were cleared to nearly the 2800-foot level. Civilian Conservation Corps crews replanted them with Norway spruce in the 1930s, but stone fences still trace pasture boundaries. The trail climbs 1400 feet in 3.3 miles, making it an easy snowshoe climb.

For the first 0.9 mile, the yellow-marked trail north and northwest from the trailhead follows an abandoned roadbed to a height-of-land at Elm Ridge. Here you reach an intersection at the edge of one of the Norway spruce stands, where you should bear right on the blue trail leading past the Elm Ridge Lean-to. The long, gradual climb follows the ridgeline, passing in and out of the spruce plantations. Eventually you pass beyond the old pastures into a forest of maple and other hardwoods. There are a few rough scrambles before you reach a sign indicating 3500 feet.

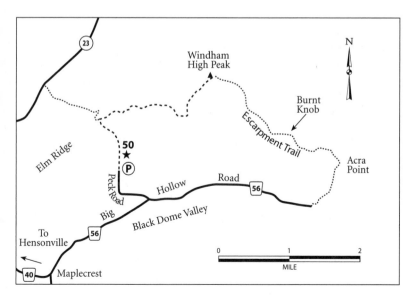

Frosted trees on the summit of Windham High Peak

There are three ledges with maintained views on the summit of Windham High Peak. The first is perhaps the most interesting to hikers, for it looks across the Black Dome Valley to the trinity of High Peaks in the Blackhead Range: Blackhead, which is the lumpish mountain on the left, and then Black Dome and Thomas Cole to the right. All three surpass 3900 feet—only Slide and Hunter are taller. Seeing them will leave you anticipating your next climb in the Catskills (see Hike 49 for directions to Blackhead).

The other two ledges look outside of the Catskill Park, and while there are no mountains to view, the distances to which you may see on a clear day—almost all the way to the Adirondacks—will astound you. The Catskill Park ends at the foot of the Escarpment, and beyond is a patchwork of farm fields, woodlots, and rolling foothills. The wilderness gives way to the cultured landscape almost precisely where the mountains end.

Allow an hour and forty-five minutes for the climb to the summit, and only slightly less for the return. Alternatively, with a car spotted at the end of Big Hollow Road, the hike can be extended by continuing southeast along the

Escarpment Trail to Burnt Knob and Batavia Kill. Several steep descents make this a more difficult snowshoe hike, but the ridge-top walk is superb. This adds another 3.7 miles to the one-way distance to make a 7-mile loop, and it adds at least another two hours of hiking time.

--*51*--
Overlook Mountain

Rating: Moderate
Round trip: 5 miles
Hiking time: 2 hours
Starting elevation: 1760 feet
Highest point: 3140 feet
Map: USGS Woodstock
Who to contact: NYS DEC New Paltz Office

Getting there: To find the trailhead, follow NY 212 west from Woodstock to the hamlet of Shady, and turn right onto Reynolds Lane. In 0.5 mile, bear right again onto MacDaniel Road and follow it for 2.6 miles to the trailhead, which is on the left at a height-of-land. This drive also offers great views of Twin and Indian Head mountains, which you will enjoy again from the summit.

All that keeps this climb of Overlook Mountain from earning an easy rating is its length, which at about 5 miles round-trip may be too long for some families. On the other hand, there is nothing difficult about this hike, which follows an unplowed access road virtually all the way to the old fire tower. Many people are drawn to Overlook each year for its unparalleled views across the Hudson Valley and much of the Catskill interior.

The hike to the summit takes about seventy minutes, but only forty for the trip back down. The grade is steady all the way, but being a road it is never steep. A 300-foot television tower near the true summit does mar the view, and it makes the mountain easy to identify from the valley as well as from other peaks.

The road/trail begins beside the register and information board, and it is such an obvious route that no further directions are needed for the first 2 miles. Just before reaching the false summit with the television tower, the road swings to the east side of the ridge and presents you with the unusual view of a three-story façade just ahead.

This derelict husk is the remains of the Overlook Mountain House, one of the famous resorts that brought civility and refinement to the Catskill wilderness. The original structure dated to 1871, but it burned in 1875. A second hotel was built on the site, but it, too, fell victim to fire in 1924. The structure that now lies in ruin on the mountain was not the victim of fire or any other physical disaster, however. Started in 1927 and abandoned in 1941 without ever being completed, it was no doubt the victim of the Depression and the outbreak of war.

The crumbling structure is never safe to enter, and at any rate there is nothing inside to see. The road hooks around the shell and past the television tower to a junction in an overgrown clearing. The trail to Echo Lake (Hike 52) continues straight, but bear right for the fire tower. The road is overarched with wind-sculpted oaks as it swings around to the observer's cabin, 2.5 miles from the trailhead.

An unmarked path leads right from the cabin to a broad open ledge with a sweeping panorama of the valley, with long stretches of the Hudson glinting in the sun. The Ashokan Reservoir is due south. Alternatively, you can climb the fire tower for the 360-degree view, and for that you need only climb to one of the middle landings. As with any fire tower in winter, be careful of ice on the steps.

Remains of the Overlook Mountain House

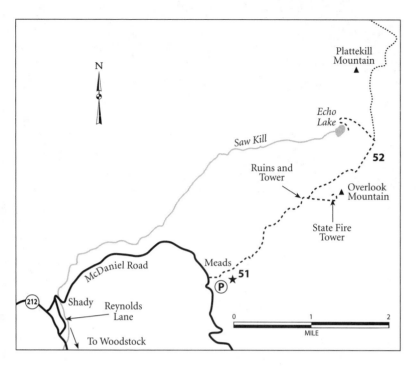

--*5 2*--
Echo Lake via Overlook Mountain

Rating: Moderate
Round trip: 9 miles
Hiking time: 4 hours
Starting elevation: 1760 feet
Highest point: 2940 feet
Map: USGS Woodstock
Who to contact: NYS DEC New Paltz Office

Getting there: To find the trailhead, follow NY 212 west from Woodstock to the hamlet of Shady, and turn right onto Reynolds Lane. In 0.5 mile, bear right again onto MacDaniel Road and follow it for 2.6 miles to the trailhead, which is on the left at a height-of-land. This drive also offers great views of Twin and Indian Head mountains, which you will enjoy again from the summit.

Echo Lake

Echo Lake is one of only two named ponds protected as wilderness in the Catskill Park. As such, it is disappointing to discover that the view from its shoreline lean-to is marred by the 300-foot television tower located on Overlook Mountain. Nevertheless, Echo Lake is a great winter snowshoeing destination, as well as an obvious way to extend the easy hike to Overlook Mountain. The route involves traversing part of the Escarpment, which is incarnated here as a flying buttress spanning the gulf between Overlook and Plattekill mountains.

The hike to Echo Lake adds 2 miles and an hour to the one-way trek to Overlook Mountain, but with an 800-foot descent to the pond that will need to be reclimbed on the way back out.

Begin the same as described in Hike 51, following the easy road/trail up the southwest flank of Overlook Mountain and past the ruins of the Overlook Mountain House. You reach a junction at 1.9 miles, where most people bear right for the fire tower. To reach Echo Lake, bear left on a blue-marked trail.

You leave behind the summit ruins and enter the Indian Head Wilderness Area, losing elevation at a gradual grade. The trail is benched into the side of the mountain; this was a carriage road constructed in 1880 to link the Overlook Mountain House with the scenic cloves to the north. Through the trees you can see the shapes of Indian Head and Twin mountains to your left, as well as Plattekill ahead of you along the Escarpment. Echo Lake itself is briefly visible in the depths of the intervening basin.

The narrow ridge of the Escarpment is overrun with oaks and laurels, with a lonely spruce here and there. One of the theories for the presence of this southern hardwood forest type in a region where northern hardwoods should be dominant is that forest fires once repeatedly burned the Escarpment over a period of centuries, eliminating the native species. Native Americans living in the Hudson Valley routinely set fires to clear the way for nut-bearing trees that provided food for both people and animals, and it is possible that their fires climbed up to the crest of the Escarpment. These southern hardwoods appear along the entire portion of the Escarpment fronting the valley, but are absent near the north end of the wall, where northern hardwoods again dominate.

The only views from the ridgeline are those you can steal from between the trees, but this part of the hike is apt to be cold as the two mountains tend to funnel wind over this ridge. At 1.4 miles past the Mountain House, you reach a marked intersection with the yellow-marked trail to the lake, which bears left and immediately begins to descend from the ridge.

The 0.6-mile descent is probably the steepest grade you will encounter, but since it follows the curve of the mountainside it still qualifies as a moderate slope. The lower section may be icy, as a number of small seeps spill trickles of water across the trail. You descend into a forest of tall beech, maple, and hemlock, finally reaching pond-level and hooking back left to the lean-to.

Since the forest encircling this round pond is open and not cluttered with brush, you may wish to walk beyond the lean-to for the view from the south shore, which does not include any towers at all, just the forested mountainside. Either way, Echo Lake is a singular destination in this region, offering an equally unique variety of natural and cultural history.

--5 3--
Hunter Mountain via Notch Lake

Rating: Difficult
Round trip: 7.6 miles
Hiking time: 5 hours
Starting elevation: 1980 feet
Highest point: 4040 feet
Map: USGS Hunter
Who to contact: NYS DEC Stamford Office

Getting there: The trailhead is located beside Notch Lake on NY 214, just south of Stony Clove Notch and the village of Hunter—in fact, the drive through the notch to the trailhead is a good scenic introduction to this hike.

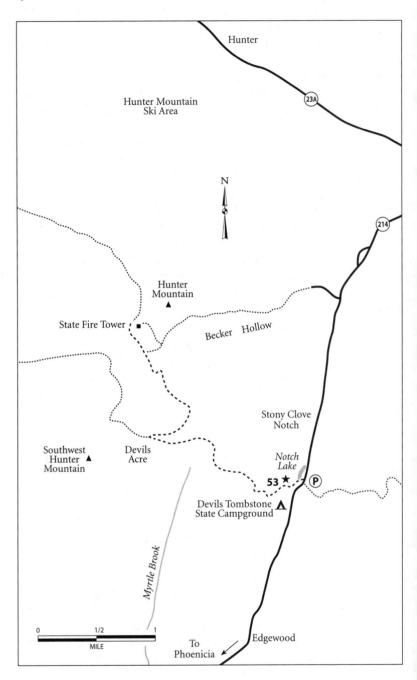

Hunter

Hunter Mountain
Ski Area

N

Hunter
Mountain ▲

State Fire Tower ■

Becker Hollow

Stony Clove
Notch

Southwest
Hunter ▲
Mountain

Devils
Acre

*Notch
Lake*

53 ★

P

Devils Tombstone ▲
State Campground

Myrtle Brook

0   1/2   1
MILE

To
Phoenicia

Edgewood

Hunter is a massive mountain that presents a number of different personalities, depending on which part you are looking at. The north side is a heavily developed ski resort; the south side is rugged wilderness; and in between is the summit, with its cozy cabin and lofty fire tower. There are perhaps twice as many ways you can climb it. At 4040 feet in elevation, it is the second highest mountain in the Catskills.

For winter hikers, perhaps the most interesting way to climb Hunter Mountain is to follow the Devils Path up from Stony Clove Notch. The trail begins very steeply, but then moderates considerably once it reaches the mid-slopes. The trail is remarkable for the many small "caves" and rock niches

Steps on the Hunter Mountain fire tower

it passes within the notch, the birch forests at the head of the Myrtle Brook cirque, and the gentle final approach to the summit. This adds up to an impressive tour of the mountain's wilderness side.

The red-marked trail begins by crossing a bridge across the outlet of Notch Lake, with Hunter Mountain beginning to rise immediately from the west bank. These lower slopes can be icy in places, especially after a thaw, and crampons may be more useful than snowshoes at first. With such a steep slope, the trail has no choice but to be steep as well, even though there are switchbacks. There is one ledge where you will need to push yourself up with your hands. While this might seem like a daunting beginning for a hike, the grade does begin to moderate after thirty minutes of climbing.

The trail swings up to follow the crest of a ridge to the head of the Myrtle Brook cirque, and then contours along the width of the cirque. The slope is steep, with a long drop-off to your left, but the trail is benched into the mountain and maintains a nearly level grade. The reason for this is quite unusual—it was the bed of a horse-drawn logging railroad. Early in the twentieth century, the Fenwick Lumber Company operated on this side of the mountain, with a hub of logging roads and cable railroads based at Devils Acre. These railroads, operated by a donkey engine at Devils Acre, helped the company harvest the timber from the otherwise impossibly steep slopes.

Ninety minutes and 2.1 miles into the hike, you reach an intersection. The Devils Path continues straight for another 0.1 mile to the Devils Acre Lean-to (a good place to take a break), but the trail to the summit bears right. This yellow-marked trail takes a steady but remarkably easy grade, in stark comparison to the start of the hike. A broad S-turn brings you into the conifer forest just below 4000 feet, and the final approach to the fire tower is like a walk down a balsam-lined boulevard.

Despite Hunter's stature, the best view from its summit is from the fire tower, which is 3.8 miles from the start. Otherwise, the balsam and spruce permit few natural views. As with any fire tower in winter, be careful on the steps if ice has been accumulating. Hunter's central location among the highest Catskill peaks gives it a spectacular view.

Opposite: The summit of Panther Mountain

THE BURROUGHS RANGE

In preparing his 1918 travelogue, *The Catskills*, Longstreth met with the pre-eminent naturalist John Burroughs and spent a day with him, driving around the Ashokan Reservoir in Burroughs' automobile. Finding little difference between the real man and the image conveyed through his essays, Longstreth characterized the relationship Burroughs had with the Catskill Mountains in this statement:

> *"The people who would dismiss him as a bird-fiend should read his book on Whitman. Those who believe that his poems are only verse might well study his contributions to philosophy. And those who would experience the inner charm of the Catskill country must know their Burroughs well. God made the Catskills; Irving put them on the map; but it is John Burroughs who has brought them home to us."*

Born in Roxbury in 1837, Burroughs pursued a number of careers (school teacher, government clerk, bank examiner) before finding his calling as an essayist and an observer of nature, rising to the status of the Catskills' most famous champion. In 1987, what would have been his 150th year, the region's highest mountain range—comprised of Wildcat, Slide, Cornell, Wittenberg, and Terrace—officially became known as the Burroughs Range.

Slide Mountain, at 4180 feet, is the Catskills' highest peak, sitting at the nexus of the Slide Mountain Wilderness Area. Its name derives from the 1819 landslide that left a scar of open rock on the mountain's slopes. Being the highest mountain, and yet so easily reached, Slide is an ever-popular snowshoe climb, enjoyed by hundreds of people every winter. A relatively straightforward trail leads up to its summit from CR 47, and it is so well used that it hardly needs any further endorsement from a guidebook such as this.

Instead, I have chosen to select a series of snowshoe routes surrounding the Burroughs Range. These are hikes that offer views of the range from neighboring mountains, such as Panther, Red Hill, and Ashokan High Point. These are vantages from which to consider the reposing, conifer-clad heights. The valley of the East Branch Neversink River offers a true wilderness hike to the very foot of the range. For those snowshoers wishing to taste the Burroughs Range proper, I have included the hike to Wittenburg Mountain, with its memorable view of Ashokan Reservoir.

Woodland Valley Road penetrates deep into the heart of what should be the wilderness interior. The Peekamoose Road severs Ashokan High Point from the Slide Mountain Wilderness, and the road through Frost Valley and Big Indian Hollow prevents consolidation with the state lands to the west. Nevertheless, the region was once even more fragmented by roads than it is currently. A turnpike once directly connected modern Denning Road with Winnisook Lake and Woodland Valley, and had this survived as a modern highway Wildcat, Giant Ledge, and Panther would have also been severed from the wilderness. Fortunately, the use of this road by vehicles was deemed impractical by area residents, and so it reverted to the status of a wide trail.

Today, most visitors to the area will find that the best access is from NY 28, which begins at the Thruway (I-87) in Kingston. This route delivers you quickly to the northern trailheads in the Burroughs Range. Alternately, there is another scenic approach from the south. In this case, take NY 17 (the proposed I-86) to Liberty, and follow NY 55 into the park. This route provides the most direct access to the southern trailheads, particularly the Denning trailhead.

One bonus about this region is that the drives to the trailheads are often as scenic as the hikes themselves. Take special note of the Peekamoose Road, connecting Rondout and Ashokan reservoirs. It takes a narrow, winding route along the foot of the Burroughs Range, passing rocky outcrops and icy waterfalls all along the way. And if you really want to see the grand view of the range, be sure to take the detour across the causeway that bisects Ashokan Reservoir. This road leads south from NY 28 at Shokan.

--54--
Giant Ledge and Panther Mountain

Rating: Moderate
Round trip: 6.6 miles
Hiking time: 4–5 hours
Starting elevation: 2200 feet
Highest point: 3720 feet
Map: USGS Shandaken
Who to contact: NYS DEC New Paltz Office

Getting there: The trailhead is located near a hairpin turn on CR 47, just over 7 miles south of the intersection with NY 28 in Big Indian, with room for about a dozen cars to park.

This route takes you over the top of one mountain, down into a col, and then up to the summit of one of the High Peaks. All of the climbs and descents involve scrambling up and down rocky ledges, but as a snowshoe hike these obstacles might at worst be described as awkward rather than difficult, especially when compared to some of the truly difficult mountains described in this book. Indeed, this is a popular snowshoe route that is followed by a variety of hikers every winter.

Giant Ledge, which tops out just over 3200 feet, is an anomaly in the Catskill Park, which is known mostly for its round-topped summits. It really is what its name suggests: a long, continuous cliff with many natural vistas over Woodland Valley and the northern Burroughs Range. Panther is a balsam-capped mountain with more limited views, but a very fine destination nonetheless.

The trail begins on the outer edge of the hairpin turn on CR 47, opposite the parking area. It begins on level ground, leading first to a footbridge over an unnamed stream. Then it begins to climb, gaining 500 feet to reach the crest of the mountain ridge. This ascent is characterized by alternating steep pitches and level terraces, culminating at the intersection at the height-of-land, less than thirty minutes and only 0.7 mile from the start.

Bear left for Giant Ledge, following blue markers. After a level respite you scramble up to the crest of the mountain, closely following the edge of the high cliffs. Allow forty-five minutes to an hour to get here. Giant spruce grow

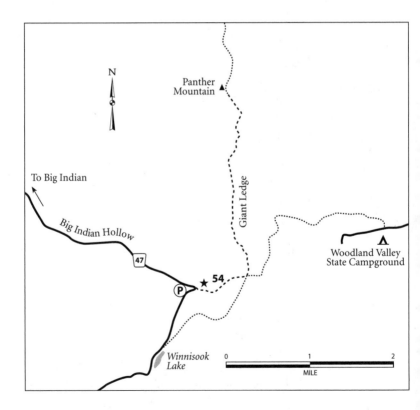

View of Cornell and Slide from Panther Mountain

from the talus pile below; the terrain seems to funnel into the upper reaches of Woodland Valley, rising on the other side to the lofty heights of Wittenberg and Cornell mountains. There are a number of very good vistas from the ledge, although the view is little changed from one to another.

The descent from the north side of the summit is a quick zigzag between rock ledges, and the initial ascent up Panther is a longer version of the same thing. Watch for a spur to the right leading to a small ledge with a view back towards Slide Mountain above Giant Ledge. The sign marking the 3500-foot level marks the boundary between the rocky ledges below and the balsam forest above, which arrives almost on cue. The grade moderates considerably after this, and the final 220-foot ascent to the summit is hardly a climb.

Panther's summit, 3.3 miles from the trailhead, is marked by a small man-made vista overlooking the Panther Kill, one of several developed valleys that penetrate deeply into the Slide Mountain Wilderness. Phoenicia village and Mount Tremper are distinctly visible beyond. The trail continues on along the ridge to the Fox Hollow trailhead, but this section is much less used, probably because the route over Giant Ledge is so much more scenic.

Allow between two and three hours to enjoy this trip up the mountains. Coming back down takes almost two hours as well.

--55--
East Branch Neversink River

Rating: Difficult
Round trip: 2.8 miles to river and back; variable beyond
Hiking time: 1–2 hours to river and back; variable beyond
Starting elevation: 2140 feet
Highest point: Variable
Map: USGS Peekamoose Mountain, West Shokan
Who to contact: NYS DEC New Paltz Office

Getting there: From NY 55 just east of the hamlet of Neversink, turn north onto CR 19. After passing through Claryville, the road becomes Denning Road and continues for another 7.3 miles to a dead end, where you will find generous parking accommodations at the Denning Trailhead.

Despite the Catskills' fame as the home of a number of world-class trout streams, very few of those waterways (or any of the major streams, for that matter) have been acquired for the Forest Preserve. One of the exceptions is the uppermost section of the East Branch of the Neversink River, which rises on the south side of Slide Mountain. The river flows through a protected wilderness valley before

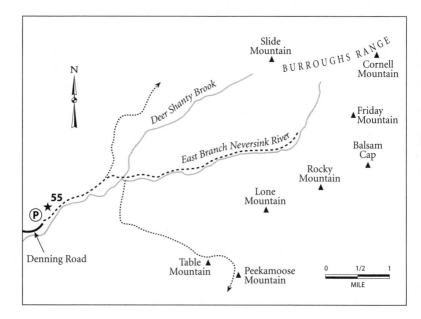

Late afternoon at the East Branch Neversink River

emerging onto private land, and as one of the precious few such valleys in the park, a snowshoe hike to the mature spruce and hemlock stands in its upper reaches is a one-of-a-kind adventure.

There is a marked trail to the river, but none follow it upstream. Therefore bushwhacking is required, and the further into the woods you wander, the better your chances for solitude. Favorable terrain also makes this an ideal place for a winter backpacking trip, and the host of High Peaks that engulf the valley may entice you to use the river as a base camp for an ascent of some of the trailless peaks.

From the Denning Trailhead, follow the yellow-marked trail into the woods. It follows the route of the abandoned turnpike to Woodland Valley, crossing private land for the first mile, with a brief interlude on one small corner of state land. After entering state land the second and final time, there is an intersection at 1.2 miles. Turn right toward Table and Peekamoose mountains onto the blue trail, which leads in about 0.2 mile to the side of the river. Allow thirty to forty minutes for this easy walk. The blue-marked trail does continue beyond the balance-beam bridge to Table and Peekamoose mountains. Those snowshoers daring enough to attempt the crossing will enjoy these mountains, which are more commonly approached in winter from Peekamoose Road.

The only bridge crossing the river as of 2005 was a single 40-foot-long log—a real balance beam. You do not need to cross the river to enjoy its valley, you need only the ability to travel off trail. How far you go depends on you. As you walk upstream, you will encounter several tributaries that could be challenging obstacles. Deer Shanty Brook is the first and largest. The river itself has multiple channels at first, but it becomes much narrower upstream, as the mountains close in to enfold the stream on three sides. It is a very attractive woodland stream, with a number of small ledges and cascades to discover.

This hike can take anywhere from a few hours to a full day—it is truly one for the explorers and daydreamers who like to set their own itineraries and follow their own whims.

--56--
Ashokan High Point

Rating: Moderate
Round trip: 9 miles
Hiking time: 4–5 hours
Starting elevation: 1100 feet
Highest point: 3080 feet
Map: USGS West Shokan
Who to contact: NYS DEC New Paltz Office

Getting there: Turn south onto Watson Hollow Road (CR 42) from NY 28A in West Shokan, and follow it for 4 miles to the parking area on the right.

The highest mountain in the Ashokan Range, south of Esopus Creek, is named simply High Point on USGS maps. However, to distinguish this High Point from others such as Windham and Kaaterskill, it is more commonly referred to as Ashokan High Point, or even Shokan High Point.

At 3080 in feet, it is not ranked among the thirty-five High Peaks. However, its position along the Escarpment and its isolation from other mountains gives it quite a view. From the summit, one can enjoy a vast vista south and east across the Hudson Valley, ranging from Kingston to New Jersey. Further northwest along the ridge, open blueberry meadows permit views of the mountains composing the Burroughs Range, with Slide itself presiding above its neighbors.

As beautiful as the summit may be, so too is the hike to the mountain along Kanape Brook. Here is one of the precious few Catskill valleys lying entirely within the Forest Preserve. The first 2 miles of this hike follow a well-defined roadbed through this valley—a section that alone recommends itself as an easy walk through deep woods, eminently suitable for both skiing and snowshoeing. The climb to the summit is moderately steep, with only a few brief scrambles over rock ledges.

An alternate descent route from the summit suggests a loop trip that entails 9 miles of hiking overall.

The trail begins across the road from the parking area, marked only by

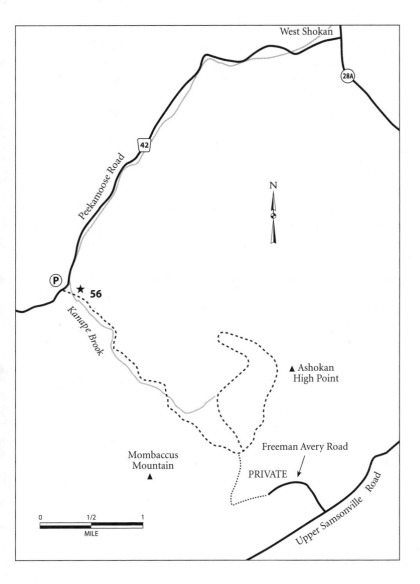

a footbridge across Kanape Brook. It takes a little over an hour for the walk to the head of the valley, but if you get an early start, take the time to enjoy the hemlock groves that shade the icy brook and the winter-only views of the mountains to the south. This was originally a public highway, connecting a small farm (the foundations of which are under the snow at 1.25 miles) with Samsonville to the south.

The trail eventually crosses the brook and climbs above it, but the grade is so gradual that when you reach the col at the head of the valley at 2.7 miles, it is a surprise to learn that you have already gained half the elevation from the trailhead to the summit. The red-marked foot trail turns sharply left here, but go forward a few yards to appreciate the abruptness with which the Catskills end at the Escarpment. The old road passes into private land a short distance beyond.

Bearing left, the trail quickly forks. The left fork will be your return route, so for now take the right fork, which follows the spine of the ridge for the easiest ascent. The trail is a narrow route etched through the oaks and laurels. Allow forty minutes for the climb from the col to the summit. The ridge rises in steps, each one seeming to be the summit until you climb to its top and see yet another rise beyond.

From the summit opening at 3.8 miles, the view is primarily eastward over the Hudson Valley. The trail bears northwest towards the blueberry meadows and the second set of views, toward Slide and its neighboring summits. The trail makes an unexpected left turn in the largest meadow, follows the wooded ridgeline for roughly half a mile, and then hooks sharply left off the mountain back towards the col. It is then just a matter of completing the easy trek back down along Kanape Brook to return to your car.

--*57*--
Red Hill Fire Tower

Rating: Easy
Round trip: 3.8 miles
Hiking time: 2 hours
Starting elevation: 2150 feet
Highest point: 2990 feet
Map: USGS Claryville
Who to contact: NYS DEC New Paltz Office

Getting there: From NY 55A near the north end of Rondout Reservoir, turn north onto CR 153. Take the first left turn at 0.2 mile, which is Sugar

Loaf Road, and follow it uphill for 4.1 miles. Here, make the sharp left turn onto Red Hill Road, and then the first right onto Coons Road, which finishes the climb onto the mountain. A sign marks the end of winter maintenance 4.8 miles from NY 55A, where there is limited parking.

There is perhaps no better introduction to the Catskill skyline than the 360-degree view from the Red Hill fire tower. This short hike is ever popular in summer, but winter road maintenance falls 0.5 mile short of the trailhead. Still, this extra distance keeps the fire tower within an easy distance for snow-shoers, and the modest grades are anything but intimidating. The fire tower has been restored, and it offers the only view from the summit. Care will be needed if you choose to climb the potentially icy steps.

At 2990 feet, Red Hill is actually a modest mountain, but the drive to the trailhead ascends much of that elevation. From the end of plowing on Coons Road, set off on foot down the unplowed road to the summer trailhead at 0.5

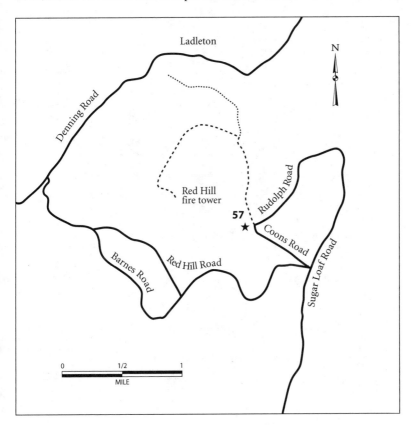

mile, where you will find the information board and register. Make sure to pick up one of the interpretive pamphlets, which will help you identify several of the tree species along the trail. The yellow markers lead just west of north, rounding several icy ledges to eventually intercept an old roadbed benched

Red Hill fire tower

into the side of the mountain. This section offers easy walking, and even when the foot trail forks uphill to the left the climbing is never steep. Large portions of these slopes were once cleared as farm pastures, extending as high as 2600 feet in elevation.

About an hour from your car, you reach the wooded summit with its observer's cabin, picnic tables, and fire tower, which was built in 1920. It is a peaceful place to rest after the short hike, but since the clearing is ringed with oaks you need to climb to at least one of the middle landings on the tower to see the graceful slopes of the Burroughs Range to the northeast, with the farm fields of Denning in the valley below. A corner of the Rondout Reservoir is visible between the hills to the southeast. Unfortunately, a cold, windy day will test your endurance—most likely sending you back to the shelter of the trees below.

--58--
Wittenberg

Rating: Difficult
Round trip: 7.8 miles
Hiking time: 5 hours
Starting elevation: 1400 feet
Highest point: 3780 feet
Map: USGS Phoenicia
Who to contact: NYS DEC New Paltz Office

Getting there: The trail to Wittenberg begins at the Woodland Valley State Campground, south of Phoenicia. From NY 28 in Phoenicia, turn south onto the unmarked street next to the Inn at Woodland Valley. In 0.2 mile you reach the bridge over Esopus Creek—turn right at the far end and then left at the Y just beyond, following the signs for Woodland Valley. It is then a 5-mile drive down the winding road to the campground. The parking area is on the right, and the trail begins to the left. There is no fee for winter use of this trailhead.

Wittenberg, which is the easternmost peak of the Burroughs Range, has one of the most scenic summit vistas of any mountain in the Catskill Park. Indeed, it seems as though the Ashokan Reservoir was created specifically to be viewed from this peak.

From the spacious parking area at the Woodland Valley State Campground,

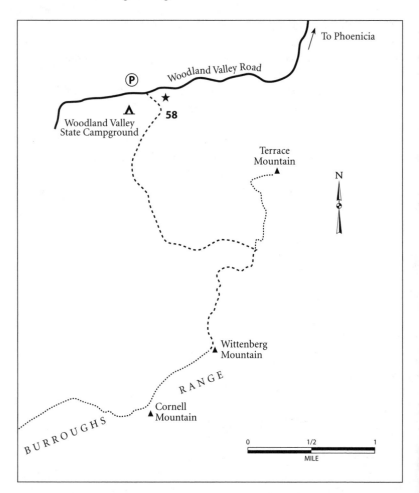

the red-marked trail cuts through a corner of the camping area to a footbridge over Woodland Creek, and you begin to climb immediately from the far end. This first portion of the trail is rocky, and there may only be a thin covering of snow—watch for ice coating the rocks. The climbing eases considerably after a few minutes and eventually levels off as it traverses the mid-slopes of the mountain, leading around the head of a high valley. For a long time, it heads east, seemingly away from the summit of Wittenberg. The forest all throughout this section is very handsome, with many tall sugar maples and hemlocks.

After hiking for ninety minutes in what seems to be the wrong direction, you reach an intersection with the original trail up the Burroughs Range at 2.6

miles. A left turn would bring you to the Terrace Mountain Lean-to, which is now at the end of a dead-end spur of the main trail. To get to Wittenberg, bear right. You are now in a forest that was logged in the past, following what is clearly the bed of an old woods road. Tanbarkers once used this route to reach the uppermost stands of hemlock on the mountain, supplying the tanneries on Woodland and Esopus creeks.

The climbing resumes at a moderate pace at first, but that ends just minutes later when you reach the foot of a steep rock wall. The trail climbs up through a cleft, which can be a difficult scramble even in summer. In winter, if necessary, you have the option of seeking a detour around to either side in the fresh snow, which is no less steep but which can be much friendlier to snowshoes. Just above this ledge is another steep pitch, though not quite as high as the first.

Beyond this, the trail continues to encounter ledges, but none as difficult as the first two. Balsam and spruce overtake the forest cover just before you penetrate the 3500-foot alpine zone, leaving just a narrow corridor for the trail. Then, more than two hours from and nearly 2400 feet above the trailhead, you

Open rock ledge on Wittenberg's summit

reach the summit's wide-open ledge and southeasterly view.

This is perhaps one of the most celebrated views in the Catskill Park. Looking down the nose of Samuels Point, the Ashokan Reservoir seems to occupy a breach in the mountain fortress wall, with massive mountains on either side and with Kingston in the distance. To the south, very little development is visible, giving the appearance of an uninterrupted mountain vastness.

Opposite: Cattails at Huggins Lake

WESTERN CATSKILL MOUNTAINS, VALLEYS, AND LAKES

Whereas the delineation between mountain and valley could not be made any clearer on the eastern edge of the Catskills, where the Escarpment rises from the Hudson Valley like a fortress wall, the western Catskills meld seamlessly into the rolling hills of the Allegheny Plateau. No one can tell for sure where one region ends and the other begins, and the Catskill Park boundary itself is merely an arbitrary line on the map that excludes several peaks over 3000 feet, including two of the recognized High Peaks.

However, before fading into mediocrity, the Catskills reach their height of wildness in the vast region between the hamlet of Big Indian and Pepacton Reservoir. Here you will find seven of the High Peaks, along with what has the potential to become the largest consolidated tract of roadless land in the park, if a few key parcels can be acquired. The variety of snowshoe routes that this region offers ranges from the remarkably easy and scenic to the challenging and wild.

The western region also contains more small ponds than the other parts of the park, although many of these are man-made. Sportsmen and wealthy businessmen established private preserves around some of these lakes, rivaling the Great Camp tradition in the Adirondacks. Some of these preserves still survive, although the state has been able to purchase all or parts of several for inclusion in the Forest Preserve. Alder Lake and Huggins Lake are both relatively recent acquisitions. Tunis Pond, at elevation 2570 feet, is one of only two natural ponds protected as wilderness in the Catskill Park.

By far, the western Catskill region is best known for its quality trout streams. This is one of several areas where fly fishing in North America took off at an early date, and indeed as you drive through such towns as Roscoe, located on the park boundary, you will see plenty of tackle shops, but few if any places selling winter hiking supplies. It is as though the residents of the town are unaware of the mountain adventures found so close to their doorsteps.

However, it is the mountains that give rise to the trout streams, and one of the most rewarding adventures in this region is the trek to the headwaters of the Beaver Kill—a rugged pass between Graham and Doubletop mountains. Roads and posted property signs follow so many miles of the Catskills' most scenic streams that it is always refreshing to find one portion of a valley that still retains its wildness.

If there is another distinguishing characteristic about the western Catskills, it is the lack of major road corridors in all but the periphery of the area. Getting there is a cinch. From New York or Binghamton, the four-lane NY 17 (the proposed I-86) passes right along the edge of the park. To the north, NY 30 traces a sinuous course around the Pepacton Reservoir, and NY 55 and 206 also skirt the edge of the mountains.

However, nearly all of the roads in between are county and town roads, which may not be consistently marked and designated as you travel from one jurisdiction to another. For instance, as you drive north from Livingston Manor toward the Balsam Lake trailhead, the road changes from CR 151 to CR 152 near Beaverkill, and then to CR 54 once it crosses into Ulster County. While most of these byways are maintained quite well in winter, the sheer number of them adds up to quite a maze. Be sure to bring detailed maps that show all of these routes, not just the principal state highways.

With so many destinations to explore and with so many long trails— many of which suggest long loops or shuttle trips—the following seven snowshoe routes should be seen as just a sample of what the western Catskills have to offer.

--59--
Balsam Mountain Loop

Rating: Moderate
Round trip: 5.2 miles
Hiking time: 3–4 hours
Starting elevation: 1980 feet
Highest point: 3600 feet
Map: USGS Seager, Shandaken
Who to contact: NYS DEC New Paltz Office

Getting there: The Rider Hollow Trailhead is located at the end of a dead-end road south of Arkville. From NY 28, turn south onto Dry Brook Road and follow it for 4.7 miles to Todd Mountain Road, a left turn. In 0.5 mile you need to bear right onto Rider Hollow Road, and follow it for another 2 miles to its end. The last section is very narrow, but there is ample winter parking at the end.

Of the four Catskill High Peaks named for the balsam fir, Balsam Mountain is the least deserving of the name. Balsams do occur as a secondary tree on the summit, but the hike up the mountain passes through so many other notable forest types that you will hardly take note of the one species for which the mountain was unimaginatively named.

All this notwithstanding, the loop over the summit of 3600-foot Balsam Mountain is an exceptional hike, with some steep grades but an overall short distance. Balsam is the northernmost point in a 17-square-mile patch of old

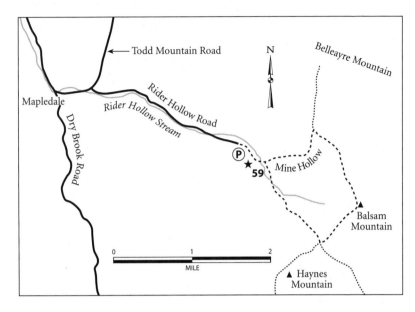

growth forest, which you will encounter along the ridgeline, with maturing second growth extending down the hollows. Farming occurred right up to the foot of the mountain, including the initial part of the hike, and limited logging occurred on the mid-slopes.

The trail begins by following beside Rider Hollow Stream, crossing one bridge and then reaching an intersection at 0.4 mile beside a second footbridge. Both forks are part of the loop, but for now bear right and cross the bridge. The Rider Hollow Lean-to is just ahead, fifteen minutes from the start.

Just above the lean-to, the trail swings across the eight-foot-wide stream, this time without a bridge. A snowshoer may encounter any number of conditions here, from a solid layer of ice to a gushing little torrent. The stream is not deep and there are plenty of stones to step on, but having waterproof footwear is essential. Expect two smaller crossings upstream, also.

As you climb through Rider Hollow, you may be puzzled by what look like large numbers of dead pine trees, like the victims of an epidemic. Actually, these are plantations of European larch, established in the late 1920s. Larches, like their North American cousins the tamaracks, shed their needles every fall, similar to the hardwoods. These plantations occupy former farm pastures, and it may seem strange to you as you climb to imagine cattle being herded over this wild mountain pass to reach the Esopus Valley (and ultimately to the markets at Kingston).

After reaching the ridgeline after seventy minutes and 1.7 miles of hiking, bear left for the trail over Balsam's summit. It takes another thirty minutes to reach the one and only vista. Note that the summit is still privately owned, although there are no restrictions on use of the marked trail. The view looks squarely on the hamlet of Big Indian.

North from the summit and back on state land, there is a steep pitch down into the broad col at the foot of Belleayre's summit. Here, look for the yellow-marked trail leading left, returning to Rider Hollow by way of Mine Hollow. Like the ascent in Rider Hollow, portions of this descent can be moderately steep. The highlight is a spectacular hemlock grove—the offspring of trees felled by tanbarkers many years ago. The trail leads back to Rider Hollow, where you rejoin the main trail and close the loop after three to four hours of walking.

Trail to Balsam Mountain

--60--
Balsam Lake Mountain Fire Tower

Rating: Moderate
Round trip: 6 miles
Hiking time: 3 hours
Starting elevation: 2600 feet
Highest point: 3723 feet
Map: USGS Seager
Who to contact: NYS DEC New Paltz Office

Getting there: From Arkville, turn south from NY 28 onto Dry Brook Road. Follow it for 6 miles to Mill Brook Road, a right turn. The trailhead parking area is another 2.2 miles on the right. The trail begins diagonally across the road.

View of the observer's cabin from the Balsam Lake Mountain fire tower

Balsam Lake Mountain is the westernmost of the Catskill High Peaks, and like many of the others it would be largely viewless were it not for its fire tower. Over the years, four towers have occupied the summit. The current one was built in 1930, and it has recently been restored with the help of a group based in northern New Jersey. It is occasionally manned even on some winter weekends, at which times the observer's cabin below is opened as a warming hut.

The trail leading to the mountain from Mill Brook Road is the popular route to the tower because of its mild grades, even though the route from the south is considerably shorter. It follows the tower's old access road, which is still lined with telephone poles. The entire route to within 0.5 mile of the summit crosses private land, confining public use to the trail itself.

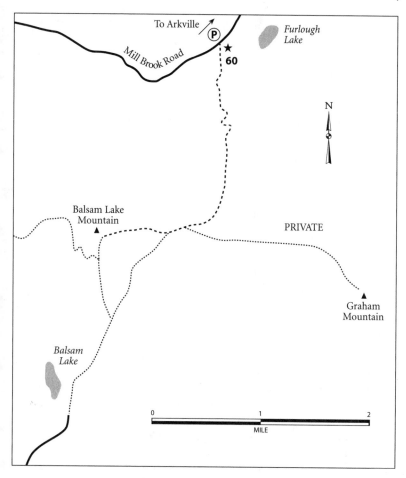

There is little that needs to be said of the first hour and 2.2 miles of hiking, which leads south along the truck trail and has modest grades for the most part. The summit of Balsam Lake Mountain is visible through the trees to your right for much of the way, although the tower is hard to distinguish.

By the end of that hour, you have reached an elevation of over 3300 feet and an intersection where the red-marked spur to the summit bears right. You now encounter several steeper grades, separated by long, almost level traverses. The final approach to the tower is through a wonderland of snow-capped balsam, bringing you first to the cabin and then to the clearing at the foot of the tower. There is no view from the ground, so you need to climb to at least one of the middle landings to see above the trees. A sea of rolling ridges spreads out in every direction.

Graham Mountain is the next High Peak along the ridge; and it is one of the four remaining peaks still on private land. As you hiked up the truck trail, you may have noticed an unmarked trail leading to the left, just before the height-of-land. People attempting to hike all thirty-five of the Catskill High Peaks use that route to reach Graham, but it should be pointed out that there is no guaranteed public access to the mountain.

Allow about ninety minutes for the climb to the fire tower, and seventy minutes for the return.

--*61*--
Alder Lake Loop

Rating: Easy
Round trip: 2 miles
Hiking time: 1–2 hours
Starting elevation: 2100 feet
Highest point: 2220 feet
Map: USGS Arena
Who to contact: NYS DEC New Paltz Office

Getting there: The trailhead is located near the point where Alder Creek Road, Old Edwards Road, and Cross Mountain Road meet 2.3 miles northeast of Turnwood. The best access is via Turnwood, approaching from the north via NY 30 and Beech Brook Road, or from the south via CR 151, 152, and 54. Cross Mountain Road, which may be plowed in winter, is a more direct route from the north, but it is an extremely rugged, cliff-side road with room for only one car at a time. It is not for the timid.

Once you manage to find the trailhead among the secluded back roads of the western Catskills, this snowshoe route is one of the easiest and most scenic in the region. It traces a loop around a man-made lake that was part of the Coykendall Estate. Except for the initial climb up to the lodge, this route contains no significant ups or downs.

There is room for several cars to park beside Alder Creek Road, where a sign marks access to the Forest Preserve. The hike begins along the unplowed access road, which climbs only 100 feet along the side of the hill to a large clearing. Here you will find the foundations of several buildings and the summer trailhead just beyond.

Coykendall Lodge still stands, although as of 2005 it was in serious disrepair and fenced off from the public. The ravages of nature and a general lack of maintenance had essentially turned the building inside out, but there are plans to rehabilitate it and preserve it as an historical landmark. It was built by Samuel D. Coykendall, a railroad magnate who purchased the lake in 1899 as a vacation getaway. Later it served as a scout camp facility until its purchase by the state in 1980.

You only have to turn around to understand why Coykendall chose this site for his camp. Alder Lake is a beautiful little pond nestled between two mountain ranges, with the valley extending to the east. A red-marked hiking trail encircles the lake, passing a number of campsites. It is 1.5 miles long and

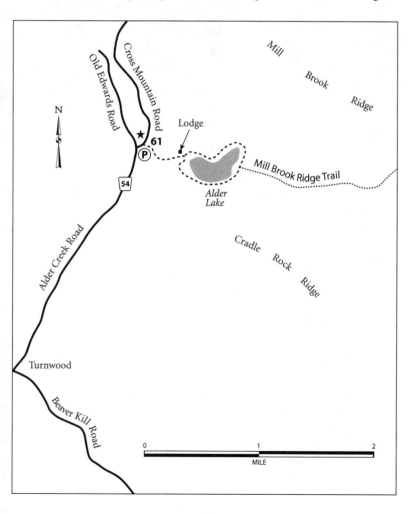

Coykendall Lodge

popular with both skiers and snowshoers. At the far end of the lake, the Mill Brook Ridge Trail takes off for its long journey to Balsam Lake Mountain.

You need only allow for a little over an hour of walking time to enjoy this snowshoe hike.

--62--
Huggins Lake

Rating: Easy
Round trip: 3.8 miles
Hiking time: 1–2 hours
Starting elevation: 1800 feet
Highest point: 2460 feet
Map: USGS Lewbeach
Who to contact: NYS DEC Stamford Office

Getting there: From NY 30 along the south shore of Pepacton Reservoir, turn south onto Holliday Brook Road and follow it for 4.6 miles to the marked trailhead on the left-hand side of the road. There is a parking area but it is not plowed; you will have to park carefully on the side of the road.

Huggins Lake is an easy walk that involves a fair amount of climbing—600 feet heading in, and 200 feet on the return. However, the entire 1.9-mile walk is along a good road grade, and so none of these ascents are forbidding. Rather, the walk to this secluded pond nestled in its own basin is a great introduction to the rolling topography and open woods of the western Catskill region.

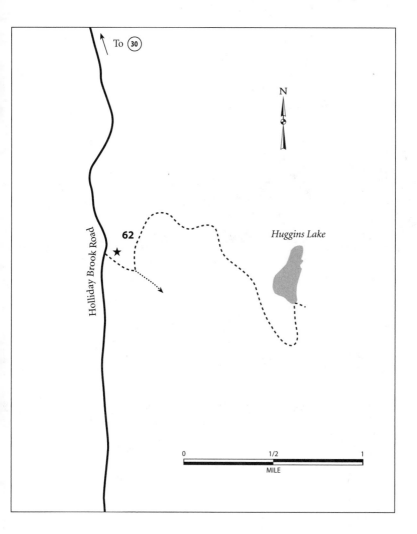

There is a register and information board at the trailhead, but the trail itself is not marked. It doesn't have to be, for the wide roadbed is so obvious that there is little chance you could lose it. There is only one turn to watch for, shortly after the parking area where a side road forks right, toward private land. The Huggins Lake trail bears hard left here, angling more northerly and beginning its climb up the ridge.

The longest climb is this first one, but the grade soon moderates as you approach the crest of the ridge. Moments after crossing the height-of-land, the entire length of Huggins Lake appears through the trees at the foot of the ridge. Rather than approaching the shore directly, the trail makes a gradual descent to the south, leading briefly away from the pond. The final pitch brings you back to the outlet of the lake, which is a man-made dam.

Cattails line parts of the shoreline, which is forested with hardwoods and a handful of hemlocks. This serene little basin is cut off from the nearest road by the ridge that you just climbed. It takes only ninety minutes total walking time to enjoy this round-trip hike.

Cattails at Huggins Lake

--*63*--
Dry Brook Ridge

Rating: Moderate
Round trip: 8.2 miles
Hiking time: 4–5 hours
Starting elevation: 1900 feet
Highest point: 3460 feet
Map: USGS Margaretville, Fleischmans, Arena, Seager
Who to contact: NYS DEC Stamford Office

Getting there: From NY 28 and 30 in Margaretville, turn south onto Fair Street. Bear right on South Side Road at 0.2 mile, and then left on Huckleberry Brook Road after another 1.6 miles. It quickly leads to a fork, where you should bear left onto Hill Road. The trailhead is located 1.3 miles further, with parking on the right.

Dry Brook Ridge falls short of qualifying as one of the High Peaks by a mere 40 feet, and that slim margin seems to be all that is keeping this from being a more popular mountain. The grades are moderate, the length is reasonable, and the views are fine. This is a very good mountain for a winter snowshoe hike, but compared to the High Peaks to the south and east it is only lightly visited.

Several trailheads give access to Dry Brook Ridge, but one of the more scenic begins off of Hill Road, on the southwest side of the mountain.

The trail starts across the road from the parking area, in a beautiful plantation of Norway spruce and red pine. Red pine is one of the most graceful trees that grow in New York, standing tall and straight, with a reddish bark that separates into delicate, flaky scales. Norway spruce is a non-native tree often seen in plantations; you will recognize it by its long cones and drooping twigs, which hang downward from the branches.

The trail begins to climb almost immediately, with grades early in the ascent that may seem trying. After walking out of the first plantation and cutting through a second, the grade moderates considerably. The foot trail first crosses and then merges with the bed of an abandoned woods road and climbs along the side of the ridge, where there are views through the hardwoods of Mill Brook Ridge to the south. The trail then narrows again, reaching an intersection with the blue-marked trail from Margaretville at 2.3 miles.

Bear right, following the trail along the ridgeline. You pass a tiny wetland on the left and dip briefly below the crest of the ridge before finally circling back towards the summit. The final climb to the top involves a few steep moments, and the trail then follows the edge of a series of rocky ledges. You pass one with an open view just minutes before reaching another near the true summit, 4.1 miles from the start.

Both views look south along the valley of Huckleberry Brook towards the eastern end of Pepacton Reservoir. The Catskill Park officially ends at the reservoir, but the Catskills themselves seem to continue uninterrupted to the horizon, melding into the hills and valleys of the Delaware watershed.

Highlights of this snowshoe route for me were watching a raven soar above the valley and getting a close-up view of a porcupine gnawing away at a beech tree. Because this long route is not as well traveled as others in the

Porcupine on Dry Brook Ridge

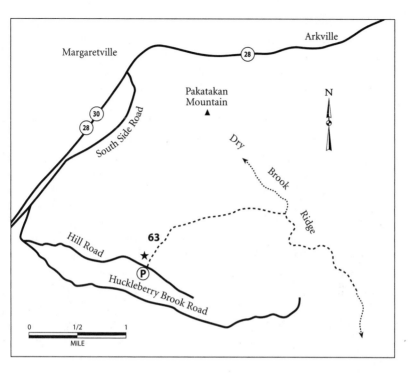

Catskill region, there is a higher probability that you will have to break your own trail on the way up.

--*64*--
Headwaters of the Beaver Kill

Rating: Difficult
Round trip: 6.5 miles minimum
Hiking time: 3–4 hours minimum
Starting elevation: 2540 feet
Highest point: Variable
Map: USGS Seager
Who to contact: NYS DEC New Paltz Office

Getting there: There are two approaches, both of them well removed from the nearest services. From the north it is possible to follow Beech Hill Road south from NY 30 to Beaver Kill Road, where a left turn will ultimately bring you to the trailhead. From the south, the best approach is along CR 151, 152, and 54, beginning in Livingston Manor, which in turn is Exit 96 on NY 17 (future I-86). Either way, allow for plenty of driving time, and note that beyond Turnwood the last 8 miles of Beaver Kill Road narrows to just one lane for long stretches. Be on the alert for oncoming snowplows.

The Beaver Kill is one of the Catskills' most celebrated fly fishing streams, and as such much of its length is posted by sportsmen's clubs and other private landowners. However, a major land transaction in 1979 added several miles of the kill's upper reaches to the Forest Preserve, in effect creating one of the largest blocks of contiguous state land in the park. In addition to the kill, a handful of small ponds and open beaver meadows are hidden in these woods, which fills the valley between Graham and Doubletop mountains to the north and the Beaver Kill Range to the south.

A marked hiking trail penetrates this valley, but in order to experience a wilderness landscape unparalleled in the Catskills you need to get off that trail and explore the valley towards the Graham-Doubletop notch. This is a route for the winter explorers for whom solitude and wide-open spaces are a key requirement. The rolling terrain and open forests are eminently suitable for

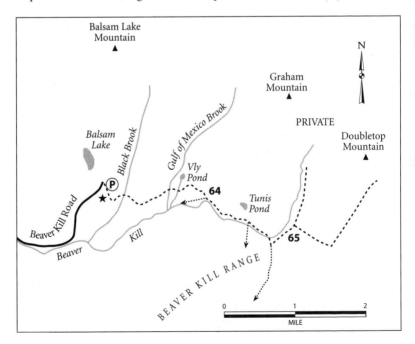

Vly Pond

winter camping, and with the 150-foot setback rule in mind you could camp just about anywhere.

Reaching the trailhead, however, invariably requires a long drive down the narrow back roads of the western Catskills. The trailhead is located at the end of Beaver Kill Road, across from the entrance to the Balsam Lake Club. The parking area is located in the corner of a field from which you can see Balsam Lake Mountain, Graham, and Doubletop.

The trail begins at the south side of the parking area, following the edge of the field for 100 yards to the register. Following yellow markers, the trail then dips to cross Black Brook on a good footbridge, traverses a wide ridge, and drops to cross Gulf of Mexico Brook, also on a bridge. The third stream crossing, which is the outlet of Vly Pond, has no bridge. The pond itself is just upstream; it is a tiny pool surrounded by a large meadow dotted with weathered stumps and snags.

The trail pulls away from the pond and at 1.5 miles reaches an intersection with a wide woods road. This is used periodically by snowmobiles to reach an inholding further up the valley. The foot trail bears left onto the road and begins to parallel the Beaver Kill, which is still a substantial stream. It is in this section that you pass close to Tunis Pond, which is hidden uphill and to the north of the trail. Its outlet is the only obvious landmark to lead you to it. Tunis has the distinction of being the highest natural, named pond in the Catskills, at 2570 feet.

At 2.5 miles the old road crosses the Beaver Kill to climb south toward the inholding, while the foot trail continues on the north bank and through a narrow glen. The stream cascades over a series of ledges here. At the east end of the glen, at 3.25 miles, the trail crosses the stream, enters the Big Indian Wilderness, and ultimately embarks on its southward course towards the Neversink valley.

At this point you should leave the trail to bushwhack into the trackless uppermost part of the valley, which is flanked by steep mountainsides to the east and west. The kill winds through a series of large meadows, and at this point it is one of the most secluded places in the Catskill Park. Its source at the pass between Graham and Doubletop remains private and posted, but enough of the valley falls on state land to allow for ample side explorations of the hills and precipitous tributaries. The valley is also a good place to begin the ascent of Doubletop (Hike 65).

--*65*--
Doubletop from the Beaver Kill

Rating: Most Difficult
Round trip: 11 miles minimum
Hiking time: 8 hours
Starting elevation: 2540 feet
Highest point: 3840 feet
Map: USGS Seager
Who to contact: NYS DEC New Paltz Office

Getting there: There are two approaches, both of them well removed from the nearest services. From the north it is possible to follow Beech Hill Road south from NY 30 to Beaver Kill Road, where a left turn will ultimately bring you to the trailhead. From the south, the best approach is along CR 151, 152, and 54, beginning in Livingston Manor, which in turn is Exit 96 on NY 17 (future I-86). Either way, allow for plenty of driving time, and note that beyond Turnwood the last 8 miles of Beaver Kill Road narrows to just one lane for long stretches. Be on the alert for oncoming snowplows.

Doubletop Mountain's distinctive profile is clearly visible from the trailhead at the end of Beaver Kill Road. Of the various approaches to its summit, this one is the longest, hardest, and perhaps most rewarding. The mountain is a 3860-foot High Peak with a densely wooded balsam summit, but with limited views. However, of its twin summit knobs, only the southern one falls on state land. Hikers wishing to explore the entire mountain must first seek permission from the landowner.

Using this route to reach the mountain can be done in a long, strenuous

Doubletop's summit

day, or it can be broken up over a weekend. If you are hiking the entire route in a day, allow anywhere from four to five hours for the ascent, and three to four hours for the return. If you would prefer to set up a winter base camp along the way, the possibilities are wide open. Tunis Pond is a scenic location near the middle point of the route, but it is possible to establish a legal campsite near a source of water practically anywhere along the way to the foot of the mountain.

Follow the route described in Hike 64 as far as the Big Indian Wilderness boundary, at a point 3.25 miles from the trailhead, and then set off into the trailless valley between Graham and Doubletop. Within the first half mile, you reach a large, open wetland on the Beaver Kill. Look for a prominent tributary flowing in from the east near the north end of the flow. It is the best guide up to the ridgeline, bringing you up to 2900 feet with relatively modest effort.

Once you reach the saddle, turn to follow the ridgeline north. Some steep climbing brings you to the 3400-foot level, but this is followed by nearly a mile of level walking through an open forest. Balsam fir is already starting to appear, but in nowhere near the numbers you will find on the summit.

You first encounter the private land boundary just before making the final climb to the summit. It comes in from the west and turns to follow the ridgeline upward. It is well marked, and it therefore serves as a guide for part of the climb to follow—which is very steep. Keep to the ridgeline, though, as it veers to the east and away from the boundary line, making the final scramble to the top through a tangle of balsam boughs.

If the fragrant air of this evergreen forest isn't enough to put miles between you and civilization, then you have come to the wrong place. There is no view, except for a hard-to-find opening near the southeast corner of the summit—consider this climb for a cloudy day.

This wooded knob shelters an active population of snowshoe hares, whose tracks you will find crisscrossing the snow. If you are alert, you may see one darting for cover, like a shadow across the snow.

The private land boundary is well marked across the summit. If you intend to continue on towards the northern summit, you will first need to obtain permission from the owner, Furlow Properties in Arkville, New York.

Appendix

LAND MANAGEMENT CONTACTS

New York State Department of
Environmental Conservation
(Headquarters)
625 Broadway
Albany, NY 12233
www.dec.state.ny.us

NYS DEC Herkimer Office
225 North Main Street
Herkimer, NY 13350
(315) 866-6330

NYS DEC Lowville Office
7327 State Route 812
Lowville, NY 13367
(315) 376-3521

NYS DEC New Paltz Office
21 South Putt Corners Road
New Paltz, NY 12561
(845) 256-3000

NYS DEC Northville Office
PO Box 1316
701 South Main Street
Northville, NY 12134
(518) 863-4545

NYS DEC Potsdam Office
6739 US Highway 11
Potsdam, NY 13676
(315) 265-3090

NYS DEC Ray Brook Office
PO Box 296
Ray Brook, NY 12977
(518) 897-1200

NYS DEC Stamford Office
65561 State Highway 10, Suite 1
Stamford, NY 12167
(607) 652-7365

NYS DEC Warrensburg Office
PO Box 220
Warrensburg, NY 12885
(518) 623-1200

Whetstone Gulf State Park
6065 West Road
Lowville, NY 13367
(315) 376-6630

RECREATIONAL ORGANIZATIONS

Adirondack Mountain Club
814 Goggins Road
Lake George, NY 12845
(518) 668-4447
www.adk.org

New York–New Jersey Trail Conference
156 Ramapo Valley Road
Mahwah, NJ 07430
(201) 512-9348
www.nynjtc.org

Bibliography

Dunham, Harvey L. *Adirondack French Louie: Early Life in the North Woods.* Utica, NY: North Country Books, 1953. 1996 edition.

Glover, James M. *A Wilderness Original: The Life of Bob Marshall.* Seattle, WA: The Mountaineers Books, 1986.

Kudish, Michael. *The Catskill Forest: A History.* Fleischmanns, NY: Purple Mountain Press, 2000.

Longstreth, Thomas Morris. *The Adirondacks.* Hensonville, NY: Black Dome Press, 2005. Reprinted from 1917 edition.

Longstreth, Thomas Morris. *The Catskills.* Hensonville, NY: Black Dome Press, 2003. Reprinted from 1918 edition.

McMartin, Barbara. *The Great Forest of the Adirondacks.* Utica, NY: North Country Books, 1994.

McMartin, Barbara. *Hides, Hemlocks, and Adirondack History.* Utica, NY: North Country Books, 1992.

Raymo, Chet and Maureen E. Raymo. *Written in Stone: A Geological History of the Northeastern United States.* Hensonville, NY: Black Dome Press, 2001.

Stoddard, Seneca Ray. *The Adirondacks: Illustrated.* Glens Falls, NY: Chapman Historical Museum, 1983. Reprinted from 1874 edition.

Van Valkenburg, Norman J. and Christopher W. Olney. *The Catskill Park: Inside the Blue Line, the Forest Preserve & Mountain Communities of America's First Wilderness.* Hensonville, NY: Black Dome Press, 2004.

Weber, Sandra. *Mount Marcy: The High Peak of New York.* Fleischmanns, NY: Purple Mountain Press, 2001.

Index

About the Author

Bill Ingersoll has hiked and back-packed throughout the western and eastern states, but he feels most at home in the grand forests of the Adirondacks. He has logged countless days exploring this vast wilderness, from the popular mountains and trails, to the many obscure places and out-of-the-way destinations that few people ever get to visit. You will find him exploring the North Country with his dog Lexie in all four seasons, by trail, snowshoe, and canoe.

In 2000 he joined long-time guidebook author Barbara McMartin in updating and revising the *Discover the Adirondacks* series, and he has now contributed to all eleven of those four-season guidebooks, which cover

The author and his winter hiking companion, Lexie

the entire Adirondack Park. He has also published articles and photographs in *Adirondack Explorer, Adirondack Sports and Fitness, Adirondack Life,* and *North Star* magazines. *Snowshoe Routes: The Adirondacks and Catskills* is his first "solo" book.

Bill is also active in the Adirondack Mountain Club, where he serves as the Wild Lands Stewardship Chair for the Conservation Committee, and where he frequently leads recreational outings into the backcountry.

When he is not in the woods or writing about them, Ingersoll works for a Utica-area bank. He resides in Barneveld, New York, and is a graduate of Rochester Institute of Technology.